JACK OF ALL TRADES

Barry Kaufman-W

Jack of All Trades

Copyright © Barry Kaufmann-Wright 2008

All rights reserved.

ISBN 978-184426-538-1

First Published 2008 by.
UPFRONT PUBLISHING LTD

Peterborough, England.

Printed by printondemand-worldwide.com

Also available from the same author

THE WILDLIFE MAN

From a very young age, 'The Wildlife Man' loved and
held a fascination with animals.
This is the story of how his passion for wildlife, originally
a hobby, became first a part of his job as a police officer,
then his full-time occupation and his life.
He is respected and admired for his work to this day. This
is a heartfelt book, and the author's passion and appreciation
for wildlife and nature is infectious.

Published by Upfront Publishing, 2002
ISBN 978-184426-026-3

Also available from the same author

RUNNING WILD

'Running Wild' is the story of a fox called Tarn who
lived on the author's farm in the early 1950s, with
steam trains on the LMS railway line, narrow boats
trading on the Grand Union canal and 3,000 free-range
chickens all on the farm.
Although this is a fictional story, some of the events
described in the tale did occur and are seen through the
eyes of Tarn.

Published by Upfront Publishing, 2005
ISBN 978-184426-327-4

Also available from the same author

CASSIE

This is an amusing story told by Cassie of her
many adventures and experiences during her very
active life, including assisting her Master in his
role as a Village Bobby

Published by Upfront Publishing, 2006
ISBN 978-184426-395-0

This book is dedicated to
William T Macdonald
'Mac'

Acknowledgements

My wife, Pat, for her patience, proof-reading skills and support in making this book possible.

John Paley for his superb artistry on the cover, back page and within the book.

Julia Smith for disseminating all my ramblings and placing them into some form of legible reading.

John Croot for checking the original manuscript.

My daughter, Georgina, for correcting spelling mistakes in the embryonic stage of the book.

All my friends and colleagues who appear in the book and made it possible.

Police work is a very demanding job – sometimes traumatic, sometimes tragic, sometimes exciting and sometimes trying – but never boring. It certainly is not a job for the faint-hearted.

Two characteristics and requirements of any police officer are unlimited patience and a good sense of humour.

This book is a very light-hearted look at policing through the experiences of the author who served with Essex Police for 32 years, through the 1970s, 80s and 90s. The book is in two parts, the first being on general policing and the second as a Police Wildlife Liaison Officer (PWLO) within the force, a position held by the author for nineteen years, before his retirement in the summer of 2005. This position was renamed Police Wildlife Crime Officer (PWCO) in 2001.

All the events are true but some names have been changed to protect the individuals concerned. All the photographs are the work of the author and some of the sketches are the work of his wife, Pat.

Index of Stories

Part One – General Policing

Joining Up

My First Posting

Suspect Person?

My Resignation?

Stop Checks Galore!

My First Driving Course

An Illuminated Police Vehicle

Commandeered

The Illegal Still

A Stolen Car with a Difference

A 'Throw Away' Comment To Regret

Poaching

Attachments

Insecure Property With A Difference

A 'Coming Together' Of Vehicles

An Apparition In The Mist

A New Beat

A 'Mini' Crime Wave

An Arsonist At Large

A Common Criminal

Green Fingers

Police Photographer

A Little Yellow Friend

A Dog With Attitude

Missing Person(s)

Goats?

Wine Galore!

Public Order Training

Miners' Strike

Police Surgeries

The Metal Detector And The Missile

An Unusual Arrest

Lights, Camera, Action

A UFO

A Missing Person With A Difference

A Christmas Bird!

Morris Dancing

Criminal Damage With a Difference

An 'Ace' Detective

An Important Prisoner

Found Property With A Difference

In At The Deep End

An Old Fashioned Pub Brawl

Drink Driving

The Warning That Was Ignored

Robbery

An Early Morning Walk

'Head First'

'Charlie's Away'

A Speeding Ticket To Regret

Robbery

An Early Morning Walk

'Head First'

'Charlie's Away'

A Speeding Ticket To Regret

Schools Liaison Officer

Part Two – Police and Wildlife

Introduction

A Monster In The Garden

A Vampire In The Bedroom

An Anaconda In The Pond

A Lion's Scratching Post

A Big Cat

An Animal With An Ear for Music

An Unusual Excuse For Being Late For Work

A Little Brown Box!

The Tenacity Of A Pair of Blackbirds

A Very Lucky Yorkshire Terrier

Whiskey Galore

An Unusual Chimney Sweep

A Toad's 'Green Cross Code'

A Scorpion!

A Kestrel, A Fox Hunt, A Rabbit and A Stoat

A Little Cottage With A Big Dog

A Determined Woodpecker

Noisy Owls!

An Owl With Attitude

An Unusual Pet

Operation Tortoise

A Pair Of Watchful Eyes

A Snake In The Kitchen

Spiders And Scorpions

Bones In The Bank

A Plucky Owl

A Stubborn Bird

Badgers

The Joys Of Public Speaking

A Crumbly Speaker

A Slide Show To Remember

Jack of all Trades

BARRY KAUFMANN-WRIGHT

UPFRONT PUBLISHING
PETERBOROUGH, ENGLAND

Part One
General Policing

Joining Up

I was raised on a small farm in the Chilterns where I developed an early interest in wildlife. On leaving school I was fortunate enough to secure a post as a keeper at the relatively new Jersey Zoo, which was opened in 1959 by Gerald and Jackie Durrell at Augres Manor, Trinity, Jersey. This was a very important time in my life and was to hold me in good stead later on as a Police Wildlife Crime Officer.

After a spell in France in 1969 with a mate, where I was supposedly studying the wildlife but in reality we were studying the bottom of a glass, I eventually arrived back in England on a Jersey States Grant to attend Writtle Agricultural College in Essex. Here I studied Agriculture and Animal Husbandry, after gaining City and Guilds Certificates in Jersey. I left Writtle with good qualifications but was unable to gain a permanent job, so I decided to opt for a change of direction in my life and applied to join the Jersey States Police. However, they were not recruiting at that time so on 6 June 1973 I was sworn in as an Essex Police Officer - I was 23 years old.

I was packed off to Police Training College at Eynsham Hall, near Whitney, in Oxfordshire for a thirteen week induction course. My introduction to the college and the military style regime there came as quite a shock. On my arrival I nonchalantly sauntered down the long drive carrying my suitcase, wearing trousers and an open-necked shirt, it was a hot day. As I reached the main building, which was very imposing, I suddenly heard a loud voice shouting behind me. I stopped and turned round and there, standing only a few feet from me, was a Sergeant, looking at me with a fierce glare. He was wearing a police flat cap, with the peak slashed to such a tight angle that the tip of the peak rested on the bridge of his nose. He had a pace stick tucked under his arm. He shouted at me, "Where's your tie, man?" I said, "It's in my case." He retorted in a shout, "Get it on now." I could see that his neck and face were flushing up red so I decided not to argue. I dug out my tie from the bottom of my case and tied it around my neck. He looked at me and asked my name, which I provided. He wrote it down in a notebook, then said, "I am Sergeant Wilson BEM, and don't you forget it, Son," before marching off with the pace stick under his arm. Our paths were to cross again in the ensuing weeks. He was the drill Sergeant, and we had a lot of drill, and a lot of him, during my stay there. The nickname we gave the place was Colditz, and my meeting with Sergeant Wilson was my introduction to thirteen weeks of blood, sweat and tears.

I was in a billet with fourteen other guys, most of whom were ex-military and, of course, were used to this type of regime. The following morning we were all on parade at 07:00 hrs. This was known as an early morning parade and was normally a punishment. Sergeant Wilson walked along the rows. Our intake were kept away from the 'Intermediates' and 'Seniors', these were the lads and girls on their 5th and 10th weeks respectively. They were inspected by Sergeant Wilson and an Inspector Bailey before being dismissed. They marched to the end of the drill square and back again, past us. They looked very impressive as they disappeared behind us.

Now it was our turn. We were brought to attention by Sergeant Wilson and then a huge man appeared at the open double doors that formed the entrance to the hall. He stood

6ft 6ins tall and was as broad as he was tall. His uniform and shoes were immaculate, and from the amount of white braiding on his cap it was obvious that he was a very senior officer. He was introduced to us as the Deputy Commandant of the centre, Chief Superintendent Hoare. He welcomed us to the centre and hoped that we enjoyed our stay there and that we learnt a lot over the next thirteen weeks.

We were then inspected by Sergeant Wilson who was carrying his note pad, which was in fact a police pocket book and, in the weeks to come, became quite infamous. The main points that were picked upon were creases in our uniforms, bulled up boots and hairs on the tunics.

When it came to my turn to be inspected, I was told in no uncertain terms that I looked like a 'Sack of ....' and I was ordered to have my beard taken off that day, only tightly trimmed moustaches were allowed at the centre. I did, however, notice that Chief Superintendent Hoare had a long handlebar moustache, but I decided not to argue. I was given the weekend to sort myself out, today being Friday. I was allocated an early morning parade for Monday morning and was given 'duty squad' that weekend, which basically meant that a group of us did not go home; instead we were security on the site. There were eight selected out of our squad, all of whom had done something wrong in the first week.

With our parade dismissed we all hit the canteen for breakfast, after which we were in the classroom where we met our course Sergeant for the thirteen weeks, Sergeant Clark, who came from the Thames Valley Force and who turned out to be a really nice guy; it was good to see a friendly face.

The first thing we had to do was to stand up in front of the group, individually and tell them about ourselves, our background etc. This was in the form of an ice-breaker; Sergeant Clark then went through the thirteen weeks workload with us.

Finally there came the dreaded little red book which contained, amongst other things, 85 definitions from Burglary to Firearms, Blackmail to Criminal Damage, Offensive Weapon to Controlled Drugs, and Infanticide to Theft. Some of these definitions were quite long. We were going to be expected to learn them verbatim in the time we were there. The book also contained the frenetic alphabet, i.e. A Alpha, B Bravo, C Charlie, D Delta and so on. We had to learn that as well, a daunting task that filled us all with dread. After our first week at Colditz we would be tested on them, then regularly throughout the course. In addition there would be a written test every four weeks, which featured lots of definitions and which we had to pass before rising to the next level at the centre. I was beginning to question my decision to join the force and so were several others. Two of the lads from Thames Valley Police had had enough; they packed their suitcases and walked down the drive, never to be seen again.

The weekend duty squad turned out to be quite a doddle. With no senior officers around we had the place to ourselves. I spent a lot of time bulling up my boots with spit and polish, literally. By Sunday night I could see my face in my boots, which was no mean achievement as my boots were not steel toe capped and were of soft leather, which I had quickly learnt was very difficult to bull up. The creases in my uniform trousers and tunic were so sharp they would have cut a steak! My early morning parade on the Monday passed off without incident. Sergeant Wilson inspected me and a few other unlucky individuals. He had noted our collar numbers in his little book and checked us over thoroughly. I was chewed off for having a small cut on my cheek -after I had lost my beard on Friday, I had to borrow a razor from a mate and had cut myself shaving. I felt that if that was all he could find fault with, I was okay.

A few days later we were all piled into a bus and taken to a local swimming pool. There was a strict rule at the centre that, firstly, if we could not swim, we had to learn quickly and secondly, we had to achieve a Bronze medallion in life-saving by the time we left the centre. The swimming instructor was the centre's fitness instructor or PTI, Sergeant Tann from the City of London Force and this was not negotiable. Fortunately I was a good swimmer and soon settled down to the swimming regime. As a warm up we had to swim what was called 'The Pyramid'. This involved swimming a length and then climbing out, performing ten press ups, another length, out, nine press ups, and so on. We had one lad who could not swim but he soon learnt with the aid of a long wooden pole with a large metal loop and my help. He was placed under my wing and by the end of the third week he was swimming a width of the pool, I was quite pleased. I gained my Bronze Medallion within four weeks and left the centre with Bronze Medallion and Bar.

Although I thoroughly enjoyed the swimming, the cross country run was not so attractive, bearing in mind that it was July/August and a very hot summer. Still we did manage to find ways of cheating and instead of a six mile run, it was far reduced. Sergeant Tann could not keep an eye on all of us all the time and a field of maize behind the centre and on the route of the run, made an excellent hiding place. On one occasion I was caught coming out of the tall crop by my favourite Sergeant, Sergeant Wilson. I was on an early morning parade for two days; I got off relatively lightly!

After a couple of weeks in the classroom on pure theory, it was time to partake in a few practical exercises. We were stopping cars, being driven by instructors who inevitably made our lives difficult to say the least, refusing to provide their name and address or failing to stop when required. The lessons learnt here were to prove useful later in our service.

I remember one incident which took us all by surprise. We had been involved in some exercises on the roads around the centre and were retuning to the hall when suddenly a Ford Granada roared up to the front entrance of the hall, across the drill square where we were situated. Two men jumped out wearing balaclavas and carrying sawn-off shotguns. They ran into the hall. Almost immediately there was the sound of two loud shots from within the building. The two men then ran out carrying their guns and one carrying a bag. They got into the car and it sped off, with thirty stunned police officers watching. One of the instructors then spoke to us and we were told that an armed robbery had just taken place and we were to return to our billets. It was the topic of conversation all evening.

The following morning Sergeant Clark mentioned the robbery and asked us to make statements about what we saw. We were told that these had to be of what we saw without discussing it with other officers in the room. There was total silence in the room for almost two hours. Sergeant Clark took all the statements and the afternoon was spent discussing the contents. The statements were then handed back randomly and we had to read them out loud individually. It was then that it became apparent that we had all written down different accounts of what had happened. Some said that there were three men and that the driver stayed in the car. This was incorrect, there were two. The descriptions of the car varied greatly from colour to make. Only a few had noted the registration number of the car, and out of them only one in our class had got it right. The descriptions of the men's clothing varied and also the descriptions of the guns were all different. Even the number of shots fired varied. In our class there were eighteen people and we had eighteen different statements. I just found it incredible.

A number of lessons were learnt from this exercise, the main one being to take statements from a witness as soon as you can after the event, whilst the events are fresh in their minds. Also, one should never assume anything - in this scenario we all fell into the trap of assuming that the two robbers were men, they turned out to be two women police officer stooges from the senior group - certain parts of their anatomy had been well disguised! I for one learnt a lot from this exercise, in fact probably more than any other exercise we did during the thirteen weeks. Lessons that helped during my service, such as statement taking and submitting, form the backbone of policing today whether it be from a witness to a road accident, or an aggrieved in a crime. Most prosecutions for whatever offence have to be supported by statements, and I was to take hundreds, if not thousands, during my career.

Marching and drill did not come easy to me. I had done very little before, only in the scouts, but my problems paled into insignificance compared to one lad from the then Mid Anglia Force. His co-ordination was non existent! His main problem was that when Sergeant Wilson shouted, "By the left, quick march," this lad would swing his left arm and left leg forward together. It looked most odd, as his whole body would rotate from side to side as he moved forward. It was most disconcerting for the officers to the side of or behind him. Sergeant Wilson kept on pulling him out and trying to teach him how to march. In Sergeant Wilson's frustration he gave the lad two early morning parades with a difference. He was to march up and down the drill square until he got it right. I thought it was a bit unfair, but to all our amazement it worked, he was marching as good as the best of us at the end.

The first four weeks flew by and at the end of this time we had a disco for the 'passing out' of the senior group who were returning to their respective forces. To bolster the number of females at the disco, two coach loads of nurses were bussed in from the Radcliff Hospital in Oxford. We had a good night, what I can remember of it! Boy, did I have a hangover the following morning? Fortunately I was on the duty squad that weekend, which was just as well. I did achieve one thing at the end of that fourth week - my boots were still giving me problems with the bulling up as it did not last long on the soft leather but one of the senior lads from Beds and Luton was returning to his force and sold me his steel toe-capped boots that shone like a mirror, so much so that you could shave in them. They cost me £1.

I was very proud of these boots and I wore them on the first parade on the intermediate group the following Monday morning, when we were inspected by Sergeant Wilson. As he reached me, he looked me up and down, and his eyes became fixed on my boots. I am not boasting but they were amongst the best bulled up boots on the parade. He walked around the back of me and I felt his pace stick lift up my uniform trousers a little way, obviously to see the top of the boot. He then walked back to the front of me and stared me straight in the eye. He couldn't give me an early morning parade for my boots that day; in fact I had no more early morning parades due to my boots. He walked on to the next officer but kept on looking back at my boots; I had a warm glow of satisfaction.

My time on the intermediate course was cut short by two weeks at the end, as my first son had been born and there were some serious complications. When I returned to Eynsham on the Monday I was a member of the senior group. Amazingly Sergeant Wilson's attitude towards us had changed completely, he became much more friendly and sociable, and this was reflected throughout the centre. I thoroughly enjoyed my last four weeks there, despite ongoing problems at home. I had cracked all the definitions - I knew them off by heart - and the alphabet. Our last four weeks were spent consolidating everything we had learnt by taking part in all manner of practical exercises.

One memorable incident occurred in our final week there. We had been threatened with fire drills throughout our stay but they hadn't happened, until now. The mustering point if the alarm went was the drill square. It was just after 07:00 this particular morning, when the alarm went off loudly in our billet. Most of us were in uniform and those that weren't soon were. We all ran out of the hut and across the grass, through the trees to the square, where we all formed up in lines, as if on parade. Some officers were in various states of dress and undress, but two officers in front of me had obviously been in the shower or bath and had come out onto the parade ground with just a towel wrapped around them - they were in the Junior intake. We all stood to attention as Sergeant Wilson and the Deputy Commandant appeared. A roll call was then taken, which took ages. I suddenly noticed that the towels on the two in front were beginning to slip; their bums were beginning to show. I could see that their hands by their sides, desperately trying to hold up the towels, which were dropping lower and lower. I heard a giggle from behind me. Mr Hoare said a few words and disappeared back into the hall, obviously to get his breakfast.

Sergeant Wilson, on the other hand, had other ideas; he decided to carry out an inspection. He walked up and down the rows until he reached the two unfortunates with their towels. He looked at them for a long time without saying anything. Then, to my amazement, he asked to see both officers' hands. They both raised their hands up to him and their towels dropped to the ground. All credit to the two, they made no attempt to retrieve their towels, but just stood there stark naked. I could hear one or two sniggers from behind me, as Sergeant Wilson spoke to the two unfortunates. His inspection continued up and down the rows and I am certain that he took a lot longer that day as the two naked men simply stood to attention.

Eventually Sergeant Wilson returned to the front of the parade said a few words regarding what was, in his view, a poor response time to the fire alarm. I felt it was quite good as we were all on parade in less than two minutes. Eventually we were dismissed and the two lads retrieved their towels and covered themselves. We were all laughing and joking about the incident for the rest of the day.

Our last week at Eynsham was good fun and the dreaded end of course exam was not as bad as expected. Inevitably there were loads of definitions and hypothetical scenarios to discuss and assess but, needless to say, we all passed. Our passing out parade was excellent and impressive and Mr Hoare addressed the parade and congratulated us all on the level that we had achieved. We then had the final march past and saluted to Mr Hoare on the podium; we had all made it! The disco that night was really good. Sergeant Clark joined us to say goodbye and we gave him a small present as a thank you from our group. We all drank well and almost drank the bar dry. I also sold my bulled up boots for £1 to a young lad on the new intake and wished him luck. The following day I returned home with a severe hangover.

My First Posting

While I was at training school I was notified of three postings within Essex and I eventually ended up at Ongar, near Epping. My Sergeant, Pete Cousins, was a real old timer. My shift partner was PC Paddy Rae, a very experienced Irishman. Both men were old-fashioned officers. Sergeant Cousins would never wear a cap in the police cars; in fact I don't think he had a cap. He would sit with his helmet on his lap; Paddy was the same. That was the entire shift, two police constables and a Sergeant. Paddy was my tutor Constable and was supposed to be with me for my first two years, that was the plan anyway.

My first couple of days were 09:00 to 17:00 duties, getting used to the station and where everything was. After this induction Paddy took me out on foot patrol with our helmets on. We walked down the High Street - this was very different to training school as people spoke to us! Paddy introduced me to many of the shopkeepers in the main shopping area and to a couple of 'tea stops'. Paddy stated that, "If you learn nothing else in this job, make sure you sort out a few tea stops for yourself." I always remembered those words - the police service runs on tea!

My first full set of shifts was seven 'nights'. The shift system in the force at that time was seven 'nights' (22:00-06:00), two days off, seven 'lates' (14:00-22:00), two days off, and six 'earlies' (06:00-14:00) followed by a long weekend off and back onto nights. On my first set of nights, Paddy and I would walk the High Street after a cup of tea at 22:00 and a briefing with the officers going off duty and the Sergeant. One of the purposes of checking the High Street shops was to ensure that all the premises were secured. We were then out on patrol in our police car, a Mini van. We had a huge area to cover, right down to the Metropolitan Police area at Chigwell and Havering. Paddy showed me around the 'Beat.' My first set of nights was fairly uneventful, but I found that sleeping during the day was difficult, especially with a young baby in the house.

When I turned up for my first duty on late turn, I discovered that Paddy had gone off sick, I believe he had injured his back, and I was on my own. After a cup of tea Sergeant Cousins told me to walk the High Street until our refreshment break at 18:00. So off I went on my very first foot patrol on my own. I was just a little nervous but as the afternoon went on I was brimming with confidence. I called into the paper shop and had a cup of tea with the owner, Brian Hubbard, who, with his brother Robert, became good friends throughout my service, as you will see as you read on.

After refreshments I was back out on foot as I had not yet been given a driving permit to drive police vehicles. This was a very valuable document, cherished by every officer. Sergeant Cousins remedied this the following day, when an examiner came down at 14:00 from HQ Driving School and I went out with him for an hour's assessment. I felt a little nervous but I passed with flying colours. This 'temporary permit' allowed me to drive police vehicles under normal conditions but not under emergency conditions known in the force as 'blues and twos'.

The final day of this series of lates was a Tuesday, and as usual Sergeant Cousins put me out on foot patrol. I had begun to enjoy these, as it gave me a chance to meet and talk to people, but my cosy existence was about to be shattered. At about 17:30 in the main street, which was busy with through traffic, I was just walking out of the road leading down to the railway station when I saw a paper boy walking in my direction along the main road. I did not think much of it when suddenly a car braked hard at the boy for no apparent reason. The car behind slammed into this car, the one behind into that one and so on - five cars in total were involved!

I went over to the accident scene with fear and trepidation. I firstly ascertained that no one was injured - luckily no one was - but as the drivers gathered around they became very heated so I had to separate them all out. I called up on my new radio, which was in two parts - a receiver and a transmitter. Each unit was about 20cm (8") long by 5cm (2") wide and 3cm (1") wide. They were very bulky and when the transmit button was pressed an aerial popped up about 15cm (6"). You had to be careful that the aerial did not shoot up your nose and cauterise your sinuses or poke your eye out! Sergeant Cousins answered the radio but basically told me to get on with it, which was exactly what I did. I issued all the drivers with tickets to produce their driving documents, and I reported all of them for careless driving. I took details of a couple of witnesses and passengers in two of the cars and, while the cars were still in situ, I marked their positions with a yellow wax crayon that I had in my pocket.

At this point a patrol car appeared, known in those days as an 'Area car', which was in fact a Ford Cortina Mk 3 that we shared with Epping. I later learnt that this crew had been requested by Sergeant Cousins to come over from Epping to see if I was okay. They assisted in measuring up the scene; traffic was building up in both directions, as only single file traffic could get through. With the measurements taken and drivers interviewed and reported, the cars that were still driveable then left the scene. Two of the cars were not driveable but we managed to manoeuvre them off the main road into the station approach road. The police station was only 100 yards from the scene so I walked back. The area car crew joined me for a cup of tea after I had apprised Sergeant Cousins of the facts. Although he didn't say it I believe he was impressed with what I had done. My first Road Traffic Accident was dealt with satisfactorily but then the mountain of paperwork began as I prepared a prosecution file - police work is plagued with paperwork

Although I had dealt with the accident fairly easily the paperwork bogged me down for ages, particularly as Sergeant Cousins bounced the file back to me three times with points I had not covered. I was rather glad to see the back of that file. As a footnote, all five drivers were convicted of 'Driving Without Due Care and Attention', including the lead driver who had stopped to buy a paper from the paperboy! I think that this was, in part, due to the fastidiousness of Sergeant Cousins when I submitted the file initially. I soon learnt that he was a stickler for paperwork; this was something we had not covered at training school!

Paddy's absence was to prove to be the best thing that could have happened to me, and I mean that in the best possible way; being on my own meant that, by and large, I had to deal with everything on my own and make my own decisions. Within my first month, I had dealt with all manner of things from neighbours' domestic disputes to poachers and bald tyres. On nights Sergeant Cousins would accompany me on the second half of the shift after I had checked the High Street. On the Sunday of that tour of nights Sergeant Cousins took the night off, he had a load of time owing. He briefed me on Saturday night as to what he wanted me to do on Sunday.

I duly signed on at 22:00 on the Sunday and had a cup of tea with the late turn officers that were going off. This overlap always proved to be very useful, as the shift going off could always appraise the shift coming on as to what had been going on - this was before the days of computers. After ensuring that there were no jobs outstanding, I put my helmet and cape on and walked off down the High Street, checking the doors as usual.

Now in those early days I smoked and, although it did not look good, I could hide the cigarette under my cape. As there was not a soul on foot, just the occasional car passing through, no-one would see. (It was different on earlies and lates). As I walked back up the High Street towards the station, I lit up a cigarette. I was less than 50 yards from the station when the radio burst into life - it was the Harlow duty Inspector and he stated that he was just leaving the station and would like to rendezvous with me. As he tailed off I saw him emerging from the back yard of the station; I did not have time to drop my fag.

He walked up to me and I saluted him, which in itself was no mean feat with a cape on. He was a short stocky man, in his mid 40s; his uniform and cap were immaculate. We stood talking for a while under the street light when I suddenly became aware of smoke coming out from under my collar. The Inspector said, "You can put your cigarette out, officer". I dropped it and stood on the stub, which was all that was left of it. On opening my cape, a cloud of smoke engulfed us both but nothing more was said on the matter. The cape was one of my warmest pieces of uniform and, on cold winter nights, I loved it; it could hide all manner of things from fish and chips to Chinese takeaways! I later learnt that this Inspector smoked, but not under his cape!

Suspect Person?

One Sunday morning I was on duty on an early turn in the front office at Ongar. I was busy doing some paperwork on my own, when there was a loud bang on the back door and I went to see who it was. I approached the door that had a large glass panel and I could see a huge man standing at the door with a Russian-style bearskin hat on his head. He was not in uniform. I opened the door and, as it opened, the man tried to barge past me; I blocked his path. At that time we were on high security alert due to terrorist activities. I said to him, "Excuse me Sir, but who are you?" He replied rather indignantly, "I am your Divisional Commander, man." I said, "I am sorry Sir, but who are you?" He shouted down to me, "Chief Superintendent Vickers, now let me in." I stood my ground, admittedly a little nervous, and said, "Can I see your warrant card please, Sir?" I think this was the final straw. He fumbled for ages in his pockets until he found it and showed it to me. I made a point of having a good look at it before I handed it back to him. He then said in a very sarcastic manner, "Can I come in now then?" I stood to one side and he barged past me. He then stopped, turned and looked me straight in the eye before saying, "I want your name and collar number", which I provided. He then disappeared upstairs; there was no one in the station except me. I grabbed my helmet and went for a walk down the High Street; I felt that I had done enough damage to my career for one day! When I returned he had gone, but there was a note on Chief Inspector Cartwright's desk from Mr Vickers asking Mr Cartwright to contact him in the morning.

The following morning at 06:00 I signed on. Paddy was back and Sergeant Cousins was on at 09:00 with Chief Inspector Cartwright. Over a cup of tea I relayed the previous day's incident to Paddy who was in hysterics, in fact he had tears rolling down his face. Paddy did reassure me that I had acted correctly and that I could not be criticised for my actions; I was not so sure. We went out in the car and, apart from a couple of business alarms activating as people came into work which were normal on early turn, the morning was quiet. We came in at 10:00 for our refreshment break, known in the job as 'refs'. Sergeant Cousins came upstairs and Paddy relayed to him the story of yesterday. He was also in tears and had to wipe his eyes with his handkerchief. I began to laugh as well; I suppose it was quite funny. I was just beginning to relax when Chief Inspector Cartwright entered the kitchen - his office was a few feet away. He looked at me very sternly and said to me, "I would like to see you in my office before you go back out." Paddy and Sergeant Cousins looked at me as I followed the boss back to his office, I was expecting the worst, my relaxed feeling had vanished. I followed the boss in and he told me to shut the door. That normally meant the worst. He said to me, "I have had Chief Superintendent Vickers on the phone this morning. I understand you spoke to him yesterday" I nervously said, "Yes, Sir." The boss asked what had happened so I relayed the story to him. By the end he was sitting in the back of his chair in hysterics. I said, "Did I do something wrong?" and he said, "Of course not, but did you not know who he was? After all he is your Divisional Commander." I said, "I have heard of him, Sir, but I had not met him before yesterday." The boss said, "Well done, nice one. Mr Vickers was well impressed." He laughed as I left his office and I felt as if a huge weight had been lifted off my shoulders. My 'incident' with Mr Vickers soon spread around the division and was the talking point for ages, but that was not the end of the matter as far as Mr Vickers was concerned, he was out for revenge.

My Resignation?

A few weeks later it was time for my first three month review with the Divisional Commander. This was standard during your first two years' probation and in those days a lot depended on them, even to the point of whether or not you stayed in the force. Now, I had learnt that Mr Vickers was not renowned for his sense of humour and I was very wary of him for, after all, my future career rested in his hands.

On the day of my review I was a little nervous, although both Sergeant Cousins and Chief Inspector Cartwright had reassured me that I had nothing to worry about. My uniform looked immaculate - I had brushed my helmet, as they do tend to gather dirt and grime out on the street. I put my white ceremonial gloves on (how things have changed!) and nervously walked up the stairs to knock on the boss's door. Sergeant Cousins opened the door and I marched in and saluted Mr Vickers who was sitting in Mr Cartwright's chair. Mr Cartwright was sitting to the left and Sergeant Cousins to the right. There was a long pause as Mr Vickers read through some papers - eventually his gaze turned to me. I looked straight ahead as I had been taught by Sergeant Wilson at training school. Suddenly Mr Vickers threw a piece of paper across the big desk in my direction and shouted, "What is this then?" I looked down a little shocked, but could not read the paper from where I was as it was upside down. Mr Vickers shouted, "Well read it, man, read it." I picked it up but was so nervous I did not really take in what was on the paper. Mr Vickers then said, "Do you really want to leave the force?" I was dumb-founded. What did he mean? I decided that I should read the piece of paper. The top title read RESIGNATION FROM FORCE - my heart sank as I read on. My name and collar number were on the form and at the bottom was my signature in standard black ink. What the hell was going on? I looked up and said, "I do not understand, Sir", suddenly all three burst into laughter. Mr Vickers took the form, tore it up and threw it in the bin before saying, "You know who I am now officer, don't you?" I said, "Yes Sir, I do." He retorted, "And don't you forget it." I said, "No, Sir."

My review went well but there was criticism of my paperwork, which was standard for probationers.

After my review I discovered from Sergeant Cousins how they managed to get me to 'sign' my resignation form, which turned out to be quite simple really. He had typed out the form and placed a piece of carbon paper between the Duty Roster and the form. The Duty Roster was a huge book where we all signed off and on duty. He had cleverly positioned it in such a way, that when I signed on duty I had in effect 'signed' my resignation as well. I did see the funny side of it - eventually. In those days the police service was renowned for 'wind-ups' on probationers, most of which were harmless fun. They developed camaraderie with colleagues and were also character building. In many respects it is sad that these practical jokes are frowned upon in today's service.

Stop Checks Galore!

One evening on a late turn, Paddy had gone to get some statements and was going to be tied up all evening. Sergeant Cousins called in two officers from our outlying village beats and I crewed up with them for the evening. They were both long serving officers with a wealth of experience and a sense of humour. I made the big mistake, which I never made again, of telling them that I had not got a lot of work on at that time - they were to remedy that on that shift.

We sat up at the Four Wantz roundabout at the top end of the town and we were soon following a car towards North Weald. The blue lights were activated and the car ahead of us pulled over into a lay-by; we pulled in behind it. I got out but the other two stayed in the warm car. I spoke to the driver who had no driving documents with him and issued him with a ticket to produce them. On checking the vehicle excise licence (tax disc), I noticed that it had expired two months earlier. The driver was reported and the tax disc was seized for evidence. I said to the two, "He had no tax", and they replied, "We know that's why we stopped him". I could not understand how they had seen it, they admitted later that they hadn't when I pressed them on it!

The next car was going a little too fast through the High Street, and we decided to stop it. I was told to warn him about his speed. Again the driver had no documents and I issued him with what we called a 'Producer'. He accepted the warning and drove off very slowly.

The next car was on the Chelmsford Road out of Ongar and was weaving all over the road. Martin and Julian both thought that we might have a drink driver. I hadn't had one yet - was this going to be my first? After the car stopped I leapt out and, to my surprise, both Martin and Julian got out as well for the first time that night! I spoke to the driver who was a senior citizen of about 90. She was very nervous at being stopped, especially as we had left the blue lights flashing due to the fact that we were on an unlit stretch of road. She could not produce her documents and I gave her a 'Producer', which confused her even more, so I had to explain in some detail what she had to do. When I asked the lady if she had consumed alcohol, she informed me that she had had a glass of wine with her daughter at lunch time. Martin and Julian had got back into the car after they had given me an assembled breathalyser. This consisted of a glass tube with crystals inside it, a mouth piece in one end and a bag on the other. I asked the lady to blow into the mouthpiece and fully inflate the bag. That started a hilarious few minutes, as I had to explain in full what was required. Eventually I did get the sample of breath, which proved negative. The lady then drove off a little confused and Julian and Martin were laughing in the car when I returned.

The next car we stopped was in the High Street and was a real wreck. We stopped it initially as both front and back lights were unlit - that was just the start. The driver was a scruffy young lad from Brentwood, who initially got quite aggressive at being stopped stating that he was being 'victimised'. I calmed him down, especially when I pointed out his lights to him - the front one was missing altogether! He then switched the engine off and got out and followed me as I examined the vehicle, a beaten up old Ford Cortina

Mk 2. The first thing I noticed was that the tax had expired by five months. The front passenger side tyre was bald but when I examined the rear tyre on the same side, it wasn't just bald it had the steel lining showing. As I took details of the second tyre, I noticed that the car was beginning to roll forward. I said to the driver, "Can you put the handbrake on, please?" He replied, "It is on." I examined the handbrake, which was on as he had said, but the car was still moving forward slowly - the handbrake wasn't working efficiently. I placed the car into gear to stop it rolling any further and went over to the police car. I spoke to the lads to see if a Vehicle Examiner was available but they had already enquired and there wasn't - it was down to me

I continued to look at the vehicle and found a few more offences in respect the general condition of it. By the time I had finished my pocket book was half full. The lad was given a producer before he drove off, a very unhappy chappie - to think that he was complaining of being victimised!

After a cup of tea we were back out again, responding to a call to a suspect white van seen in the Toot Hill area, outside some houses. The residents in the village were on a high level of vigilance after a speight of dwelling burglaries in the area recently. As we shot up there, this was part of Martin's beat, we passed a white van travelling in the opposite direction. We spun around and went after it, and caught it in Stanford Rivers where we stopped it. The result was that it was all in order - it was a delivery driver making a very late delivery. He was given a producer and the informant was advised of the result.

The last car of the evening was a speeder in the High Street. Two young lads were tearing through the High Street, well in excess of the speed limit. We managed to stop them at the end of the High Street when we had recorded the speed of the vehicle as 54 mph in a 30 mph speed limit! The driver thought it was a big joke, until I reported him for excess speed. His attitude changed and when I examined his driving licence I understood why, he already had two endorsements on his licence and was, therefore, facing disqualification; he was what we used to term a 'totter.'

We returned to the station where I was dropped off and Sergeant Cousins asked me what I had done through the evening. I had a hat full of offences to sort out once the producers came back. I saw Sergeant Cousins wink at Julian and Martin as they left. The end result of this evening's work was that the first car we stopped with the out of date tax disc also had no insurance - a serious road traffic offence. The old lady had no test certificate for her car. The lad with the Cortina, in addition to all the offences on his car, also had no insurance and was disqualified for nine months with a substantial fine. The speeder was disqualified for six months as a totter.

My First Driving Course

It was not long before a vacancy on a four week driving course came up, as someone had to drop out. It was offered to Ongar and Sergeant Cousins grabbed it and gave it to me. These courses were like gold dust and I snapped it up. It was a residential course at HQ Driving School. There were 21 people on my course and we were divided into squads of three with an instructor per squad who remained with us throughout the course; our instructor was Sergeant Charlie Woods. We were driving a variety of cars from Ford Cortina Mk 3 to Triumphs. There were many memorable incidents on this course but I will relate just a few.

The first was involving one of our squad - I will spare his blushes and not mention his name! We were on what we called a day run and were heading for Kings Lynn in Norfolk. We were travelling under what was known as 'Response' conditions, in other words with blues and twos. We were travelling very fast on a long, straight stretch of road in the Fens. Way ahead of us we could see some crows in the middle of the road, apparently feeding on a dead rabbit, as they have a habit of doing. We were bearing down on them fast when all of a sudden the driver took both hands off the wheel and flicked his hands in front of him saying, "Shoo, birdies, shoo." Sergeant Woods looked across and calmly said, "Who's steering this ****** car?" We were in hysterics in the back. Needless to say this driver had to buy the teas at the transport café.

One of the elements on this course was to become proficient on the skid pan. This was great fun but obviously, like everything on this course, there was a very serious side to it as well. We had to do controlled skids all around the pan. The cars we were driving were Ford Cortinas, Mk 2 and 3, with bald tyres. The skid pan had an oily substance on the surface called sure slip. The combination of the two made for a lethal surface that you could hardly stand up on. Once you got the hang of it the controlled skids were not too difficult and although we all managed to turn the cars right round a few times, this was not the idea!

One memorable incident on the skid pan, which involved a misunderstanding, left a lasting impression on the pan. We were engaged in controlling a four wheeled skid. To create the skid we had to drive down the ramp, onto the pan, and then brake and control the subsequent skid. When it came to my turn I sped down the ramp and onto the pan. As I ended up on it, I hit the brakes then, very gracefully, slid as in a slow motion ballet, right across the pan and up the 20' high bank the other side, coming to rest at the top. This was followed by a very carefully executed reversal back down the bank, to the loud protestations from Sergeant Woods standing in the middle of the pan. When I reached the pan I looked back up the grass bank and there were two beautiful skid marks right up to the top. I won't repeat the comment from our instructor - I had hit the pan at about 35 mph when it should have been 15mph! The marks that I had made lasted for ages; I was quite proud of them.

The other incident I recall involved a chase on the M2 in Kent. We were on a day run down to Dover in a very powerful Triumph. The car was unmarked, but of course we were in uniform and I was driving my one hour leg of the journey. I should just mention that there was a national 50mph speed limit due to a fuel crisis but we were exempt. I was in the centre lane doing about 65mph when a Jensen Healey sports car went past us as if we were standing still. Sergeant Woods looked at me and said, "Come on son, get after it." I needed no encouragement, a quick change of gear and heavy right foot down and we were off. We had a police radio in the car and Sergeant Woods called up to our control room who in turn passed it on to Kent Police. It was always difficult to stop cars in unmarked police cars.

We eventually caught up with the Jensen in the middle lane; it was travelling at 110mph! We drew alongside it and I saw that the driver was an old lady. The two lads in the back put their hands up to the window, showing five fingers and said, "Fifty." She obviously misunderstood this and waved before suddenly accelerating off, leaving us way behind. I then saw in the mirror the blue flashing lights of a police car that was racing down the fast lane. I pulled over and they sped past, acknowledging us as they did so. They were soon up behind the Jensen and as we went past they were pulling her over on to the hard shoulder. Back at training school much later I had to submit a statement, which was sent to Kent traffic.

At the end of the course we had a final assessment with an examiner from the driving school, normally an Inspector or above and we all passed. Before leaving Ongar I was to successfully pass an advanced course and I also passed the test to drive personnel carriers.

An Illuminated Police Vehicle

When I first arrived at Ongar the only police vehicles we had were a police Mini van with no roof lights and an unmarked Ford Escort Mk2. We also shared an area car with Epping - a brand new Ford Cortina Mk3.

Soon after returning from my driving course I attended a number of incidents whilst on nights where a blue flashing roof light on the Mini would have been useful. In particular I remember one incident when I was dealing with a fallen tree, on a blind bend, in driving rain.

I raised the issue with the Sergeant and he suggested that I submit a report outlining the problems that I had recently experienced, particularly with the fallen tree. The advantage of a blue light is that it warns other drivers of a potential hazard, whether it be an accident or a fallen tree. If ever you want anything in the police service you have to submit a report.

A few weeks after my report went in I was told that HQ had agreed for a blue light to be fitted; our van was one of the first in the county to have one. In those early days the flashing light consisted of a static bulb mounted to the roof with a silver reflective disc that revolved around the bulb. The whole assembly was encased in a clear blue plastic cover, which clipped into place.

Everybody thought this was great and I was the hero of the hour but my time of glory was short lived. One morning I was detailed to take the van to the Harlow Divisional Traffic garage to collect a colleague who had dropped off a vehicle for service. A brand new car wash had been installed and as the van was a bit dirty I decided to put it through the wash.

The huge rollers began to move across the bonnet of the vehicle. I watched, thinking that the Sergeant would be quite pleased that I had cleaned the vehicle. The rollers with the long nylon strands then moved up on to the roof. Suddenly, and without warning, the blue light cover came flying out of the wash with such force that it hit the brick wall behind me and shattered into a thousand pieces. The silver reflector and the rest of the mounting followed as I rushed into the wash to stop it; I was too late. The entire assembly had disappeared, leaving a gaping hole in the roof through which the water was pouring. The mechanics in the garage were in hysterics as I stood there with the crumpled and smashed remains of the blue light in my hands. How was I going to explain this to the Sergeant?

To add insult to injury the mechanics could not replace the light immediately so I had to ring the Sergeant to arrange for transport back to the nick for myself and my colleague. The Sergeant himself came over in the CID car. When I explained what had happened he couldn't stop laughing, especially when I showed him the 'remains'. After that incident a memo came out stating that "All police Mini vans and Mini saloons fitted with new roof blue lights must NOT go through the automated car wash." I did not live it down for quite a while!

Commandeered

Police officers have the power to commandeer a vehicle in an emergency and we are covered by Crown Insurance. I was to exercise this power one late turn afternoon while I was on the High Street. I was at the bottom of the High Street on foot patrol and about to call into one of the shops for a cup of tea, when the radio suddenly crackled into life. I was being sent to an Injury Road Accident on the zebra crossing at the other end of the High Street, over quarter of a mile from where I was. Paddy was attending court in Epping so I was on my own - I knew that if I ran it would take a while.

I saw a beige coloured Austin 1100 coming down the hill with a woman driving. I stepped into the road and stopped the car. I spoke to the lady and said, "This is an emergency. There is an accident at the other end of the High Street and I need to get there in a hurry. I am commandeering your car." Without a word she got out and ran around to the passenger seat and got in. I jumped in and roared off up the street. The lady said, "Isn't this exciting?" (It was probably the fastest that her car had ever been driven!) Within a very short space of time I was on the scene. I leapt out and thanked the lady who moved round to the driver's side and drove off; I never did find out who she was. An ambulance arrived on the scene just after me, and the injured lady on the crossing was taken away. Her injuries were not too serious; she had stepped out in front of a car. I took all the details of the driver of the car and of witnesses. In those days all injury accidents had to be reported to HQ.

An Illegal Still

One early turn, Paddy and I were having our first cup of tea of the day at 06:00 after talking to the night shift going off duty. The phone went - it was our control room at HQ. Customs and Excise were raiding a property on our beat, where it was believed that there was an illegal still producing a type of Polish Vodka, and they had asked for our assistance. They were hitting the bungalow at 08:00. We arranged for the Customs team to call in at the police station first so that we could be briefed on exactly what they had got and what role we were playing.

The team of three, two men and a women, met up with us and we discussed what was happening. It turned out that there was going to be very little for Paddy and I to do. We left the station and soon arrived at the bungalow - we had to move fairly quickly. Our brief was that Paddy and I would go to the back of the property to seize anyone trying to leave the bungalow but no-one did.

Eventually the back door opened and the Customs team came out followed by a little old man who looked at least 70. He was pale and looked very apprehensive. We all walked down to a large shed at the bottom of the garden, which the old boy unlocked. I then discovered what a real life still looked like. It was a huge and complicated mass of pipes, tubes and glass demijohns. The shed was also full of crates of bottles, stacked from floor to ceiling, full of home made vodka. The old boy readily admitted what was in the bottles and that he had made it.

The contents of the shed were photographed in situ and then the entire shed was taken away by the Customs team with us assisting in loading it up. A neighbour had come in to sit with the old couple who really were quite frail.

With the van loaded up, and the old boy reported for the offences by Customs, we all left. Paddy and I did get a little taster of the vodka, which was like fire water. It removed the back of your throat, but it was nice! The old boy's wife had shopped him to Customs after a domestic dispute; she now bitterly regretted her actions. I couldn't help feeling a little sorry for the couple.

A Stolen Car With A Difference

For a number of months we were plagued with stolen cars on our beat, some being dumped and others stolen. All the cars were either Mk 1 or Mk 2 Ford Cortinas. They were being dumped, undamaged but out of petrol. The intelligence we had indicated that all these thefts were down to one young man in Brentwood and it was inevitable that he was going to get caught before long. There had been some high speed chases involving this young man but he had escaped capture every time - his luck was to run out quite dramatically.

One evening Paddy and I were out in the car when we received a call reporting a car in a ditch on the North Weald road out of Ongar; we were soon on the scene. It was a Ford Cortina Mk 1, completely on its roof, deep down in a water-filled ditch. We gave Control the index number of the car and it came up as a stolen vehicle from Brentwood. A number of police cars then joined in the search for the occupant(s), the engine was very hot suggesting that the person(s) responsible might still be in the area. One officer decided to check the car parks and estates in Ongar, just in case we were about to lose a car, as this had all the hallmarks of our car thief. We couldn't get the tracker dog as it was involved in another incident in Harlow.

Paddy and I remained at the scene awaiting recovery of the vehicle. Eventually a recovery vehicle arrived and after some discussion it was decided to lift the vehicle out of the ditch and turn it over on the road. The chains were attached and the lift began. I was shining my torch onto the car and as it rose up I suddenly saw a person underneath; I shouted to Paddy. The lorry continued lifting the car and suddenly a young male ran off along the ditch. Paddy saw him and took a flying leap off the top of the ditch and crashed down on top of him. He ended up flat in the ditch with Paddy on top. I rushed over as Paddy got off him and we handcuffed him before we placed him in the police car. It was a miracle that he wasn't injured and had managed to get out of the upturned car.

The lad was later identified as the suspect from Brentwood who had been stealing all our cars and, although initially he wasn't talking to us, he later admitted to numerous car thefts.

A Throw Away Comment To Regret

One morning I left Paddy in the station doing paperwork while I went out on patrol. Sergeant Cousins sent me to a boundary dispute between neighbours over a hedge line. I arrived at the bungalow concerned and spoke to the gentleman. As a result I followed him through to the back garden. Along the boundary was a line, in excess of 100ft, of Leylandii trees that were over 25ft high. They were excluding a lot of light from the garden and that was the issue that was bothering the elderly gentleman and his wife. The trees were on their neighbour's boundary, right up against their fence.

Unfortunately this was what we used to call a 'domestic' issue and not a police matter. I had a cup of tea with the lovely couple but I had to inform them that it was not a police matter and that they should contact their Solicitor. They appreciated the advice and as I walked out of the house, I made a throw away comment that could have cost me my career. As I said goodbye I just happened to say, in a very jovial manner, "Of course, a copper nail in every tree would kill them very quickly", and I laughed as I walked away.

I never thought any more of the matter until I returned to the old couple's bungalow some three months later at the end of a long, hot, dry summer. I had called to see them on another matter altogether. They had witnessed a road accident whilst out in their car and I called on them to get their statements but as they greeted me, the gentleman said, "You're the officer that came about those trees, your copper nail certainly worked, come and have a look." My heart sank into my boots as I walked through the bungalow and out into the back garden. The sight that greeted me was absolutely incredible. The Leylandii were still there but every one was dead. It was a line of brown, from the very bottom to the tip of every tree; I was flabbergasted.

Rather shocked, and feeling quite worried, I went back inside and had a cup of tea with the couple before taking their witness statements but all I could think about was those trees. I said to the gentleman in a rather shocked voice, "What did you do?" He replied, with a laugh, that the neighbour had gone to Australia to see his daughter for three months and while he was away he had gone round there with a hammer and a tin of copper nails. He had knocked four nails into each tree in a ring. When the neighbour returned a couple of weeks ago, he had assumed that the dry summer had killed them and he was having them taken down shortly. I said, "What if they find the nails?" The old boy said, with some confidence, "They won't." I never heard any more on this matter despite sweating for quite a while and I never made a throw away comment like that again.

Poaching

As the autumn rolled in my work load began to vary from road traffic offences, which were always regarded as the bread and butter offences for probationers, to crime and poaching. Ongar is in a rural part of Essex and the Epping/Ongar section included a large section of Epping Forest. We also had the electrified Central Line underground, a line spur between Epping and Ongar. This line attracted a lot of poachers for rabbits and, although this should have been dealt with by the British Transport Police, we were normally the first officers on the scene and ended up dealing with the incident. It was often a dangerous activity as we pursued the poachers along the live line, but Paddy and I had a lot of success along here, particularly on Sundays on earlies when there were less trains operating.

Pheasant poaching was also a problem from the early autumn to Christmas. Many of the larger farms and estates in the area employed gamekeepers, and we worked closely with them as my keen interest in wildlife and rural crime became well known in the area.

One memorable incident involved poachers early one Sunday morning, just before Christmas. Paddy and I had just finished dealing with a stolen car from an estate in

Ongar, when we were sent to a poaching incident on a farm between Ongar and North Weald. Control had received a call from a local gamekeeper who was watching a gang of men through binoculars; they were shooting pheasants on a big scale. In view of the fact that firearms were involved Paddy decided to call up for assistance, as we set off for the location.

We were en route when we were redirected to a white van on the edge of a field. This was believed to belong to the poachers, as it was where the men had gone to and were currently being challenged by the gamekeeper and a few of his colleagues. A fight had broken out as the poachers tried to make their escape. We arrived at the same time as two police cars from Epping and a traffic car arrived. In the field tempers were lost on both sides so we all rushed in to calm the situation down.

I grabbed one of the poachers, who was about to throw a fist at the keeper, and the next thing I knew I was on the ground rolling around in the mud with a very strong man; it was all I could do to restrain him. He struggled and tried to hit me but eventually I was sitting on top of him putting the handcuffs on, which was proving difficult with all the slippery mud on my hands. When I looked up, Paddy was marching another man off in handcuffs. As he passed me he smiled and said, "Are you okay?" I stood up leaving the man in the mud - he wasn't going to go anywhere with his hands secured behind his back. He was swearing and shouting at me. Eventually I pulled him to his feet and as I did so he tried to kick me. He was placed in the back of the area car and the crew were not entirely happy about having a filthy, dirty prisoner in the back of their newly valeted car. Sunday morning early turn was the car cleaning shift, but I had no choice.

Eventually all the men were arrested and taken off to Epping Police Station while Paddy and I were left at the scene to get the witness statements. We all adjourned to the gamekeeper's cottage, where we had a cup of tea and a bacon butty, while we took the statements. I was covered from head to foot in mud and my uniform was soaked, but I couldn't get home to change. We took the statements over to Epping where the men, who were all from Kent, were eventually charged with poaching offences, firearms offences and assault on police. I was the only one to get assaulted that day.

Attachments

During the first two year probationary period, a probationer was expected to complete a number of attachments to various departments within the force. These included attachments to CID, Traffic, Coroners Officer, Crime Prevention and Administration Departments.

My first attachment was to the Harlow Divisional Coroners' Officer for two weeks, during which I was to attend twelve post mortems. I found them fascinating - I have always been keen on biology. The pathologist knew this and made it very interesting for me. Most were carried out at St. Margaret's Hospital, Epping. This was a good attachment as it was 09:00 to 17:00, but I did get called out one evening to join the Coroners' Officer, who picked me up from home to attend a body in a wood at Nazeing. This transpired to be a suicide by drugs overdose. I went to this post mortem and I also attended two inquests during this attachment. The only post mortem that I found difficult was on a two year old boy who had drowned in a garden pond, he was the same age as my son.

My next attachment came soon afterwards and that was a six week service with the Traffic Department. My partner for this period was a very experienced traffic officer, PC Derek Foster, based at the Harlow traffic garage in Old Harlow. This was very interesting as the work varied from escorting abnormal loads to dealing with fatal road accidents. We had three of these in one week and a sudden death on the M11 between junctions 7 and 8. This call came in as a fatal RTA but the M11 at this point was still under construction. Attending it was interesting as we weaved in and out of machinery and debris. We found the car down a hole where the central reservation would eventually be. The driver was a motorway worker who had suffered a major heart attack, whilst driving off the motorway.

We also had some exciting high-speed chases after stolen vehicles. One was abandoned on the A414 en route to Hertford. We both gave chase across the fields, after the driver who had made off, and I caught him with a very impressive rugby tackle in amongst some trees. He bruised his shoulder on one of the trees as he crashed to the ground; he was a big man. The car was stolen from Chelmsford.

I recall one amusing incident when Derek and I were on a late turn. Halfway through the evening we got called to a 'suspect on premises' at a bungalow in North Weald. On our arrival, Derek suggested that I went to the back of the property in case anyone tried to make off from there, while he went to the front. I stood in the back garden in anticipation for what appeared to be an age, but no-one appeared. Suddenly I heard a low voice from the other side of a fence calling, "Barry, Barry. Where are you Barry?" It was Derek - I had gone into the wrong garden! Fortunately there was no-one on the premises, the old lady had heard a noise and thought someone was breaking in, just as well that they weren't! Sergeant Cousins called me a few things when he heard about it a few days later.

Another incident I will never forget was when we had to deliver what we call in the job an 'agony'. Two children had been staying for a weekend with their grandparents in the West Country. The children had been killed in an horrific road accident and we had to inform the children's parents. I was to learn throughout my service that these jobs were often the most difficult aspect of policing. Young recruits would often ask what the most difficult part of policing was assuming it was the blood and gore but I would always reply that it was delivering an agony message. There is no easy way to do this, even after 30+ years in the service.

We also had a couple of disqualified drivers and half a dozen drink drivers, and I managed to get a hat full of bald tyres and other vehicle faults. I had plenty of paperwork by the time I returned to Ongar.

My next attachment was to CID and I had some unexpected bonuses. Firstly, I thought I was going to complete this attachment with Harlow CID, but at the last minute I was told that I could remain at Ongar and work with the local detective, DC John Gartland. This attachment was supposed to be for four weeks but ended up as three months. The reason for the extension was that a murder enquiry in Grays had taken half the CID strength at Harlow so John and I ended up covering. We had a busy time with a few credit card frauds and a couple of burglaries that were passed to us to deal with. A team of pickpockets from Brighton were arrested up at a football match between Harlow and Leicester; John and I ended up dealing with them.

However, the highlight for me was one morning when the Harlow Area Car had been called to a suspicious death at a high rise block of flats in the town. Almost immediately CID was requested to attend. John was in court so I attended with a young detective. What we found was, to say the least, interesting. The flat had been occupied by a man who was senior in years and an eccentric recluse who kept himself to himself. Because of this no-one thought anything of the fact that he hadn't been seen for months. The area car crew had forced entry at the request of the gas board, who needed to check the supply, and immediately called us. What we found was simply a skeleton laying on the bed. There was no smell and no flies although the floor was covered in dead flies. There was a mountain of junk mail by the front door. Scenes of Crime Officers attended along with the Coroners' Officer. A post mortem revealed that there were no suspicious injuries. I had to appear at the subsequent inquest and an open verdict was recorded on the poor old boy.

My final attachment was two weeks on admin, which I found really boring and irrelevant. Fortunately during my second week I managed to get a few days out with the Scenes of Crime Officers which was much more interesting - fingerprinting, photographing crime scenes and searching for clues. At that time I felt that this might be a niche for me in the future.

An Insecure Property With A Difference

After being away from Ongar and shift work for quite some time, it took a while to settle down again. My first week back was on nights and I was back on the street again, checking properties until midnight every night. Halfway through this tour of nights I was becoming very tired, as I was not sleeping during the day. I was walking down the High Street, testing all the doors simply by turning the door handles and leaning against the doors. On reaching the butcher's I was falling asleep on my feet. I pushed down the door handle and leaned against the door, which flew open. I went crashing in and I fell down the three steps leading into the shop, ending up in a spread-eagled slide across the sawdust covered floor. My helmet came off and rolled across the floor. Fortunately I didn't hurt myself but I felt a real idiot. I got up and brushed myself down, then looked around to make sure that no-one was watching. I went back outside and closed the door. I called up on the radio - the aerial of the radio narrowly missing my nose - and spoke to Sergeant Cousins who arranged for the key holder to attend. All was in order in the butcher's shop, the gentleman made no comment on the human shape in the sawdust!

On returning to the police station for a cup of tea at midnight I had a long chat with Sergeant Cousins in the Sergeant's office before we went upstairs to the kitchen. Sergeant Cousins followed me up the stairs and halfway up he said, "I see that the butcher's floor is now nice and clean", and burst out laughing. I hadn't noticed that the back of my uniform was covered in sawdust - get out of that one!

A Coming Together Of Vehicles

One early turn I was out in the area car with PC Jimmy Johnson from Epping. We were cruising around some of the back roads in the south of the section, on the border of the Metropolitan Police District. It was a dull, misty morning and so far had been fairly quiet, but that was all set to change.

As we came around a sweeping bend we saw a car approaching, it was a Ford Cortina Mk 2 with two youths on board. The car sped by us but I did manage to note its registration number. Fortunately the Police National Computer (PNC) had just been launched and, although its services were quite limited in those early days, cars could be checked. While Jimmy was turning the car around I checked the number and it came up as stolen from Romford overnight - the pursuit was on.

The Cortina driver had spotted us turning around and had made off at high speed, we were not far behind. I was giving a running commentary as we followed the car, the purpose of this being that the controller could direct other police vehicles to our location. We had blues and twos operating and the noise in the car was quite deafening.

We were speeding through the lanes for what seemed to be an age, until we came up to a T-junction leading onto a major road. The car shot out without slowing down or any regard for other road users; fortunately it was clear. We stuck with him as we drove through Abridge, with pedestrians stopping to watch. I don't know what speed we were doing - all I knew was that it was fast! Some skilful driving by Jimmy kept us in contact with the car and the two in the car were looking very nervous, as every attempt to lose us failed. We were now travelling extremely fast towards Chigwell and Met land!

We came down the long hill past the Metropolitan Police Sports and Social Club at Chigwell. I was giving a running commentary to our control and was advised that other cars were en route to assist with stopping the Cortina. We continued into Chigwell and I saw a police car half across the road in the shopping area blocking our path, I thought that we had got him, but did not expect what happened next. The driver of the stolen car had obviously seen the road block. The car started to slow down and we were expecting what was known in the job as a decamp, which basically means that the occupants would run away from the vehicle, but what happened next totally surprised us. The car suddenly turned into a large bus/railway station on our left but we stayed with it. It shot through the area, narrowly missing a number of parked cars and a bus which was just pulling out, and back out onto the road that we had just left, travelling back the way we had come. From the smoke coming from the tyres of the car, it was under severe acceleration. We kept with it, passing two Met cars travelling extremely fast in the opposite direction.

We followed the car back up the hill, past the social club, and on towards Abridge. After passing over two roundabouts, the second roundabout led off towards Loughton and we were back out in the country. At last we saw an opportunity to attempt to overtake the car; we pulled out and eventually drew alongside it, we were going extremely fast. I looked at the driver and passenger of the car and they looked at me; the passenger gave me a two finger sign.

Almost immediately the car rammed into the side of our car. There was a violent jerk of the police car and a horrible sound of scraping metal. Jimmy managed to control our car and turned it into the stolen car - we were still locked together. Both cars swerved to the left and the stolen car crashed into a ditch. As we were still locked in we came to an abrupt halt, thank goodness for seatbelts! Johnny leapt out but I couldn't as my door was pressed up against the other car. The occupants of the stolen car were trapped in the car. I climbed over the gear stick and got out just as a number of Met cars arrived. The occupants of the stolen car were going nowhere.

A breakdown wagon was requested and arrived fairly quickly. Our police car was pulled out of the ditch and away from the stolen car. The occupants were then removed from the stolen car and the Met lads allowed Johnny and I to make the arrests, although the car was stolen from the Metropolitan Police area. We took them into Romford with the assistance of two Met cars. After making our statements about the pursuit we were taken back to Ongar whilst our car was taken to our HQ at Chelmsford. Sergeant Cousins gave me a wry smile and said, "Well done". The following morning I was called up to the chief Inspector's office and had to give him a full account of what happened, at the end he congratulated me. I was summoned to see the chief Inspector about a month later and was shown a letter to our Chief Constable, Mr Nightingale. It was a letter of thanks from the senior officer at Romford, apparently the two we arrested were prolific car thieves from their area that they had been unable to catch. They had been responsible for over 50 car thefts over recent months and other offences including burglary, street robbery and one was wanted for questioning regarding a rape of a 14 year old girl.

This was a good result for us and the car was repaired and back on the road fairly quickly.

An Apparition In The Mist

M y final good arrest came just before I left Ongar. I was on nights on my own as Paddy was on leave. Johnny Johnson had been sent over to pick me up in the area car; I was to be his observer for that tour of nights. We had a fairly quiet tour of nights until the last one, which was a Sunday night. After our cup of tea at 22:00 I went down town as usual to check the properties, while Johnny came over with the car. A fog was beginning to descend and, by the time I got back, visibility was down to about 50ft. It was unsafe to patrol in this so Sergeant Cousins instructed us to remain on standby at the police station. This suited me as I wanted to clear my outstanding paperwork.

As the night went on the fog got thicker and thicker and I thought we were going to have a very quiet night, but I was wrong. At about 05:00, an hour before we were due to go off duty, the fog began to lift slightly and Sergeant Cousins instructed us just to go and have a drive around for the last hour.

We patrolled around very slowly but apart from some early morning commuters arriving at the underground station, there was very little happening. We drifted out into the country and Johnny decided that we would check a local golf club house that had been burgled a couple of times recently.

As we travelled down the lane leading to the club house it was light enough for Johnny to switch the lights off the police car. As we drew close to the front of the building I saw a large van parked at the side with its rear doors open and loads of boxes inside. Almost immediately a large male appeared at the rear of the van carrying a box. He saw us, dropped the box and ran off. I leapt out and gave chase while Johnny put out an urgent assistance call before following me. The man was running across the golf course, I could only just see him in the mist. To my surprise I was catching him quite quickly and, with a rugby tackle that the England front row would have been proud of, I brought him to the ground on the very wet grass. I handcuffed him while Johnny went racing after another male that had appeared from the building.

I then had a problem, I had arrested one but there were obviously others involved. What was I to do with this one? I couldn't see Johnny but I heard shouts coming out of the fog. As I escorted my man across the golf course and we came up to the back of the clubhouse, I knew that Johnny would have locked the police car around the front, but I desperately needed to go after the others. I then spotted some steel railings, which were about 6ft high, surrounding a small staff car-park. I had a brainwave - I would handcuff him to the railings. I took one cuff off threaded it through the railings and back on to his wrist. After ensuring that he was secure, I went off into the fog which was still quite dense.

I had only gone a short distance when I met Johnny coming towards me out of the fog with a male in handcuffs; Johnny wasn't very tall and the man towered over him. I spoke briefly to Johnny and then went off into the mist again, towards the river where he believed another had gone. After running a short distance, I suddenly heard Johnny shout, "Barry, behind you." I turned around and I could hardly believe what I was seeing as an apparition was emerging from the fog. The man I had arrested was running across the golf course in the fog with a long section of the railings held high above his head!

I ran after him and quickly caught up with him. I shouted for him to stop but he ignored me so I had to rugby tackle him for a second time. He hit the ground with a loud clank as his head hit the bottom of the railings. I was soaked through and muddy from head to foot. I escorted him back to the police car with the railings still attached. The man was shouting something about police brutality as Johnny placed his prisoner in the car. By this time other police units were arriving, including a German Shepherd tracker dog from the Met. My man was removed from the railings and placed in another car.

After ensuring that someone was going to remain with the cars I went off with the dog and his handler. As we walked through the dense fog the dog suddenly became very excited and began to track. We broke into a run but after a short distance we came to an abrupt halt at the bank of the river. The dog cast around but had lost the scent, it was obvious that our quarry had gone into the river.

The dog and his handler went off in one direction and I in the other to comb the bank. I had only gone a short distance when I spotted a hand holding onto some rushes on the edge of the bank. I called the handler back as I pulled a man from the water. He was very cold and shivering violently, he looked totally dejected. As I arrested him, he said, "Am I glad to see you?" The handler lent me his handcuffs and I led the dripping, shivering man back to the cars. A fourth man had been picked up walking along a lane on the other side of the golf course - we had got the lot. Before Johnny and I left to follow the men in, we spoke with an official from the club and he showed us why the alarm had not activated, they had sprayed foam into it - not possible these days with modern alarms, just in case you are thinking of trying! They were all taken to Harlow Police Station but I couldn't understand why I was the only police officer who was covered from head to foot in mud, even Johnny was fairly clean except for his boots. After making our statements Johnny and I went off duty.

I was off for the next couple of days and returned for a late turn on the Wednesday. The Chief Inspector was in his office with the door shut - I don't know why but this was something I always checked when coming on duty. After a cup of tea, Sergeant Cousins told me that the boss wanted to see me. Not knowing why he had requested this I gathered my thoughts before knocking on the door; Sergeant Cousins was right behind me. I was beckoned in to be met by Chief Superintendent Vickers sitting at the desk and the Chief Inspector standing by the window, Sergeant Cousins joined him. I was busy racking my brain thinking what I had done wrong!

Mr Vickers then boomed out, "You did a good job on Sunday, but how did you find them?" Nervously I went through the sequence of events, including the handcuffing of my prisoner to the railings and the subsequent re-arrest, to which he and the others burst out laughing. Mr Vickers then went on to explain that, not only did the four admit this burglary, but also the previous two. The big bonus as far as he was concerned, was that they also admitted to a large number of similar burglaries on golf clubs in the south east, over a three year period. He congratulated me and said, "Well done Son, a really good bit of old fashioned police work." I looked up at the two standing behind him and they both had their thumbs up. Mr Vickers then told me that my personnel file would be updated with a commendation from him. This was my first and I was quite chuffed. After Mr Vickers left, the Chief Inspector called me back upstairs to congratulate me and to tell me that this was praise indeed from Mr Vickers, who was not known to be generous with his compliments. I came out of his office on a real high. Johnny and I were the talk of the station for a while - I just thought that we were doing our job!

A few months later my probation was confirmed, I had made it. Both Sergeant Cousins and the Chief Inspector knew that I was interested in getting a detached beat (a village beat). I was raised in a very small village with a local 'bobby'. Two local beats within the Ongar section had come up but I was unsuccessful then one morning I was summoned to the Chief Inspector's office to be told that a vacancy had arisen on a detached beat at Thaxted, within the Great Dunmow section. Was I interested? I did not know Thaxted or the area, but I expressed an interest and was told to go and have a look. When I finished at 14:00 I raced home, picked up the family and drove out to Thaxted in our Mini. The house was brand new and was having the final touches, including the central heating, installed.

I contacted the Chief Inspector at 09:00 the following morning and told him that I was definitely interested. Two days later I found that I had been successful and we could move in three weeks, I was absolutely delighted.

A New Beat

We moved in to the Thaxted police house with comparative ease, although the builders were still doing some finishing touches. My arrival, wildlife interest and my connections with Jersey Zoo were soon reported in the local press and the Thaxted Bulletin. The first few weeks were spent settling in and meeting people; I would walk the beat every day with my helmet on and I soon earned the nickname 'Barry the Helmet'. There was also a car exhaust centre run by 'Barry the Exhaust' and a tyre centre run by 'Barry the Tyre' - it was a very small community! A police officer walking the beat was a sight that the community had lost and people would make a

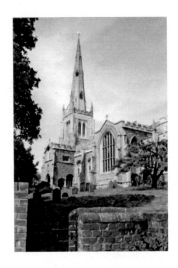

point of coming up to me and talking. It was amazing how much information was forth coming from these little chats.

Alongside the regular police service there was the 'Special Constabulary', comprising unpaid volunteers who wore uniforms similar to ours and were invested with full police powers for the area to which they were appointed. Thaxted had its very own 'special officer', Dave Kinnley, who I soon met.

He was a ranking officer, with the equivalent rank in the regulars of a Chief Inspector. He was a huge man, 6'6" tall and wide with it; in uniform he looked very imposing. We became close friends and he regularly accompanied me, on weekends and when I was on a half night duty. We were to become involved with all manner of incidents, as you will read as you move through this book.

My new Chief Inspector was based at Saffron Walden Police Station and came over to introduce himself. We got off to a good start when he said to me, "I will put my cards on the table by saying that in my view village beats are a luxury that the service cannot afford." I thought that this may not bode well for me; he did however assure me that he would support me in my new role.

The police office was attached to the house and was accessed via a door from the house. I soon learnt that as a village bobby, you were expected by the public to be on duty 24 hours a day. The most regular callers at the office were for production of driving documents, found property and enquiries for directions. Most of these could be dealt with fairly quickly and I rarely booked the time (policing on the cheap was common then). The police car I was to patrol in was a Mini saloon, with a radio! However, it had no blue light on the roof, a situation I soon remedied and it became one of the first saloons to get the blue roof light.

A Mini Crime Wave

Within a few weeks of arriving at Thaxted I was to experience the activities of a 'problem family' in the town. Typically, I was 'weekend off', which meant that I had Friday to Monday off work.

On the Friday morning I received a call that someone had set fire to the British Legion Hall and the trees adjacent to it were on fire. The fire brigade were en route and when I arrived I found the Leylandii trees next to the hall ablaze, and the end wall of the hall was alight. The fire brigade were all ready there and were putting the flames out. I took a look around but there was no-one there apart from a few onlookers. The local patrol car from Dunmow attended and I returned home.

On Saturday morning a report of a burglary came in from a bungalow owned by a lovely old lady that I had got to know. She rang me and was very upset so I went down to see her. In the burglary she had lost all her jewellery. I was curious as to how the burglar had got in, but all soon became clear. We found that a small window had been forced open and the back door had been unlocked from the inside. The conclusion was that someone very small had got through the window and had opened the back door, so at least two burglars were involved. The local car from Dunmow and CID attended, and once I was satisfied that the old lady was okay I went home.

At about 10:00 on Sunday I got a call that three suspects had been disturbed at a burglary at another bungalow in the town. I immediately attended and spoke to the elderly couple who had returned from church to find three youngsters in their property. They had run off out of the back door empty handed. A number of police units attended including a tracker dog, but they were not found. However, Dave Kinnley had a word with me later and gave me the name of a family in the town that might be responsible for all this activity, the notorious Wilson family. I went home.

On Monday I was due to start work at 17:00 but that was set to change. At about 11:00 I got a call from my control to say that two old ladies had been robbed in Orange Street by three youngsters. I attended and found the two ladies being tended to by an ambulance crew. A police unit was already on scene. Apparently the three youngsters were wearing balaclavas and the ladies didn't know who they were, but I did!

I left the scene and went straight to the Wilson's house. The three boys, David the eldest at 12, Chris at 10 and little Paul at just 7, were there. Lo and behold they had just got home and curiously on the kitchen table were three balaclavas. Their parents were there and I informed them of what I suspected the boys had been up to over the weekend, I arrested David and Chris but Paul was under age. I called for back up as I wanted to search the house. This search of the boys' bedrooms revealed an Aladdin's cave of suspected stolen property, including the jewellery from the burglary on Saturday, a wallet from the second on Sunday that the couple had not realised had been stolen, and the contents of the old ladies' handbags.

They were taken to Dunmow Police Station along with their parents who brought Paul in as well. I suspected that he had been put through the window at the first burglary and my suspicions were confirmed - they all admitted their involvement with the fire, burglaries and the robberies. In view of their ages they were all cautioned.

These boys became responsible for a lot of crime in Thaxted over the years, David and Chris in particular.

So much for my weekend off, but my bosses were pleased with the outcome.

An Arsonist At Large

Soon after I arrived at Thaxted I was to get embroiled in a major operation. It had become apparent that we had an arsonist at large, in the east of my beat, after a number of thatched houses were badly damaged or destroyed. It was a miracle that no-one had been injured, or worse. The difficulty for me was that most of the fires were started in the middle of the night, always on the night of a full moon and most of the attacked properties were in remote areas. The two villages concerned were Hempstead and Great Sampford, both of which were spread over huge areas. Those local residents who had thatched properties were living in fear and were calling us to investigate the slightest sound outside. In an effort to try and catch the person(s), I started to work a lot of half night duties, normally finishing between 02:00 and 03:00 and Dave would often accompany me. Initially, it had been left to me to catch the arsonist but that was to change.

After a six month spree of fires with no real indicator as to who was responsible, it came to a head when we had three thatch fires in one night. One of these involved a dear old lady living in a remote thatched cottage, who was saved by a passing milkman who risked his own life to save her. This was the last straw and a meeting was ordered with CID and a number of senior officers to set up an operation to try and catch the perpetrator(s). Over one weekend all the residents of the two villages were interviewed using a questionnaire. This involved drafting in a large number of officers from HQ and cost me a fortune in tea at my office, which was the rendezvous point. One name kept on cropping up during these interviews, so much so that it was decided to place this person under CID surveillance. A month of these observations produced no credible evidence against this individual.

At the same time that these observations were under way, another operation started involving cycle patrols through the night with no lights fitted. The main area of these patrols was a lane over three miles long extending between the two villages. Three officers would commence riding from one end and three from the other end. This was a very dark lane with overhanging trees at various spots. One of these patrols will always stick in my memory.

We had met up at my office at 22:00 and taken the bikes out to the two villages in a van, which we had on loan from HQ for the operation. The cycle patrols commenced at midnight, using the striking of the church clock at Hempstead to synchronise the start. We had no lights on the bikes, relying on the moon for light. This particular evening I had started from the Great Sampford end with two officers drafted in from Harlow. Our ride started with a steep, uphill ride of nearly half a mile, which nearly killed my Harlow colleagues. The full moon cast eerie shadows across the narrow lane as we continued on. My two colleagues did not like the fact that there were no street lights and as we rode on they grew more nervous. Their anxiety grew when a vixen called with that haunting scream, one of them stopped and shouted, "What the hell was that?" I had a job preventing them from turning around and riding back!

On and on we rode, the occasional dog barking in the distance was normally a good indicator of where the other three riders were - on this particular night it was a Detective Sergeant from Saffron Walden and two police constables from Harlow. A tawny owl hooted and swooped across my two PCs on silent wings, I thought that was going to be the point that they turned back but I managed to persuade them that owls are harmless. As we reached the half way point on a very dark, sharp bend with trees meeting in the middle, I guessed that the other three should not be far away, but I had misjudged their speed. All of a sudden there was an almighty crash of metal and shouting as the six bikes collided and we all ended up in a ditch with the bikes on top of us. The silence of the night was shattered by swearing and shouting, which eventually turned into hysterical laughter as we all picked ourselves up. Fortunately, apart from a few scratches, no serious injuries were incurred. The incident report for that night made interesting reading! I never saw my two Harlow PCs on the operation again.

On another occasion, while still on the operation, Dave and I were out in my brand new police vehicle a Mini van, which replaced my Mini saloon. We had called in on a friend at Hempstead who lived in a remote thatched cottage. It was midnight and he made us a cup of tea as he was pleased and comforted to see us. After leaving him we patrolled slowly around the village. As we approached a junction we saw a car turn towards us and, as it approached, its lights suddenly went out. This seemed very suspicious so we turned around quickly at the junction and began following it. At that point its lights came back on and it sped off. We gave chase, although the pursuit was very short. At a sweeping left hand bend the vehicle veered off the road, through a field gateway and into the field, with us immediately behind.

As expected, three occupants (two men and a woman) decamped from the vehicle. The men were lost in the dark but the woman was trying to run through the ploughed field in high-heeled shoes! I leapt out and grabbed her, while Dave disappeared. I brought her back to the van and placed her in the back. She was very drunk and her language was choice. I then called for back up, as I had been told on the radio that the car had been stolen earlier that night from Colchester. Dave then returned to the van. I had requested a tracker dog and one had been dispatched from Suffolk Police as we were right on the county boundary and the Essex dog was miles away. I tried to talk to the woman, but she was very abusive so I gave up.

A few minutes had elapsed, when suddenly we saw two men, covered in mud, walking towards us out of the dark. Dave and I got out and, as they approached us, one said, "Do you want us, Guv?" We arrested them and they were placed into the back of the van, making a real mess of my new vehicle! I informed my control that the three were now in custody and to stand the Suffolk dog down. Soon afterwards we were joined by another police unit and, after a brief chat, we left them with the stolen vehicle to arrange recovery while we took our three in. It was at that point that I was informed that there was no custody Sergeant either at Saffron Walden or Great Dunmow and I was directed to take them to Braintree Police Station, some 24 miles away.

On the way to Braintree I noticed in the mirror that one of the men was trying to manoeuvre the two bars that secured the back doors - obviously he was going to try and jump for it. I put my foot down and sped through Braintree to the old police station. I roared into the back yard with the three in the back falling over one another. Before they had chance to escape, I had reversed the car tight up against the wall so the doors would not open. I left Dave in the van whilst I fetched a number of officers to assist with removing the three from the vehicle. I rolled it forward and they were removed, the woman still swearing like a trooper. As one of the men walked past me, he said with a smile on his face, "You weren't going to let us jump for it were you?" I smiled back and said, "Nope."

The end of the arsonist operation came fairly abruptly when our main suspect was arrested for a minor theft, miles from the attacked villages. Whilst in the cell at Saffron Walden he asked to see me and CID. I was off duty at the time but went in to the police station, as this could have been important. During the subsequent interview he admitted all the fires and some other thefts. He eventually appeared at Chelmsford Crown Court, amidst a mass of media coverage. He appeared before Judge Melford Stevenson, and he was sent to Broadmoor secure unit indefinitely; the local community were very relieved.

A Common Criminal

Soon after we had caught the arsonist we started to have a spate of thefts in the same area as the fires. Barns and garages were being hit, mainly at night. As well as the usual property being stolen, such as chain saws, electric drills, mowers and strimmers, we were also losing bags of cement, tarpaulins, wheelbarrows, hammers and nails. I began to look around for someone doing some building work!

Over the next six months or so the mini crime wave, as it was described in the local press, increased to the point that every day thefts were being reported. From the enquiries that I made, one name kept appearing. It belonged to a man working on a local farm and living in a tied-cottage, where he seemed to be doing some building work. It was also curious that all the farms in the area had been hit except the farm where he was working – what a coincidence! Furthermore it transpired that this man was regularly visiting the market at Bury St Edmunds, where he was placing items for sale.

I decided to sit up and wait for him early one morning. I positioned myself on the road out of Hempstead towards Steeple Bumpstead, on a day before the market was due to take place, for it was then that sale items needed to be entered. The first few times I sat up, concealed in a field gateway hidden by a high hedge, nothing happened. Then early one beautiful, sunny morning I was in my usual spot when I saw a pick-up truck, belonging to the man, travelling fast in the general direction of Haverhill with a tarpaulin covering the contents in the back. I pulled out and began to follow him. He obviously saw me behind him and accelerated away, but I stayed with him. He slowed down in Steeple Bumpstead and, at a suitable spot, I put my blue light on and indicated to him to pull over. I thought he might make a run for it but he slowed down and stopped. We both got out and he appeared very nervous. We had a brief conversation: I asked him where he was going he replied, "I'm going to see a mate in Haverhill." I then asked him to lift up the tarpaulin, as I wanted to look in the back. He became extremely nervous but I insisted. As the sheet rolled back I saw I had struck gold, for in the back were six chainsaws, four motor mowers, a short, brand new, galvanised ladder and a new strimmer that was so clean I don't think it had been used. There were a number of other items and I said, "What's this lot then?" He replied, "It is my mate's and I am taking them back to him." I said, "I don't believe you, I suspect that this lot is stolen." I then arrested him and placed him in the back of the Mini van. I was later joined by the Saffron Walden area car and the observer drove the truck back into the police station.

The man was not happy at being caught but later admitted that the property on the truck had been stolen by him, even the tarpaulin covering it up! A subsequent search of his house revealed an Aladdin's cave of stolen property including cement, wheelbarrow and an assortment of tools. His garden shed looked like a show room at a garden centre. There were about a dozen chainsaws hanging up neatly in rows and loads of other electrical and garden equipment. It turned out that people were calling at his house to purchase these items; it took me ages to sort it out and get it all identified by the various owners. My man had been very busy!

The final tally of offences detected was 103, which included a number that had not been reported. Due to the number involved and the value, which ran into many thousands of pounds, he was sent for trial at Chelmsford Crown Court. He eventually appeared before His Honour Judge Peter Greenwood and pleaded guilty. In sentencing him the judge said, "You are nothing but a common criminal and I am going to hit you where it hurts." He was fined just under £1,000 and the judge told him that he had narrowly avoided a custodial sentence; however he had taken into consideration that he had fully cooperated with the police and pleaded guilty saving a lot of court time.

Green Fingers

I was to have another case up before His Honour Peter Greenwood at Chelmsford Crown Court, involving a case of cultivating cannabis.

The case came to light when I was asked to assist the DC at Dunmow CID with a raid on a house where it was suspected that the resident was cultivating cannabis, which at the time was illegal. Armed with a warrant the two of us visited the premises early one morning. In an upstairs bedroom we found 42 pots with healthy cannabis plants growing. We seized the pots and the man was arrested. We had to get scientific proof that they were in fact cannabis plants and once this had been obtained, the man was charged.

The man had previous convictions for the same offence and because of this he was sent to Chelmsford Crown Court for trial. Now, in those days, for evidence of cultivating cannabis we had to produce the growing plant if possible, this was known as primary evidence. This basically meant that we had to keep the plants growing. They were placed in an office at Dunmow Police Station and the DC and I had to keep watering them.

The watering system worked well as we had a rota until the August of that year when both of us went on annual leave at the same time. The DC thought that I had arranged for someone to water the plants and vice versa, the end result being that the plants received no water for over two weeks. When we returned to the office, the sight that greeted us took some believing. All the plants had died and all the brown leaves had been shed all over the table and floor, leaving tall 'sticks' in the pots. After a lot of deliberating we came to the decision that we would bag up all the leaves and produce them with the pots, hoping that the court would accept our 'remains' as evidence.

At the trial, the accused man was pleading guilty so I was the only officer to appear to give antecedents. The pots were all lined out on a table below the judge with the bags of dried leaves nearby. I got up into the witness box ready to read the antecedents before the judge passed sentence. I glanced down at the exhibits and the judge did the same. He then looked at me with a slight smile and said, "Officer, you do not have green fingers do you?" I replied, "No, Your Honour," I was not going to go into detail. The few people in the court, including a few barristers and the defendant, laughed as they all looked at the 'sticks'.

The defendant received a suspended prison sentence and a substantial fine. The judge made a Destruction Order on the exhibits and as he did he said, "It looks as if the officer has done a reasonable job already." The judge then rose and left, I gathered up the exhibits and left the court, with one or two sarcastic comments from the barristers as I went.

Police Photographer

With living on the beat, so to speak, it meant that I was on duty 24 hours a day. People regularly called at the office or phoned me. Late one evening I was sitting watching TV when there was a loud knock at the house door. A very anxious member of the public was reporting a serious road accident on the main road out of Thaxted towards Dunmow.

I grabbed a coat and cap as it was pouring with rain, ran around to the police car and sped off. The ambulance, fire brigade and a flying doctor were already at the scene when I arrived. There was a car on its roof across the road and a lot of attention was being given to the driver, who was trapped and very seriously injured. Eventually he was removed from the car but shortly afterwards he died in the ambulance.

The ambulance eventually left along with the fire service, leaving me and another local car at the scene, holding the fort until an accident investigation unit attended from Police HQ. A police recovery unit was also requested to take the vehicle to HQ for examination. While we waited I took a few photos to add to my collection, which I use for a road safety lecture for secondary schools.

As I was taking the last of the shots, the investigation unit attended with the recovery unit. I didn't recognise the officer and he didn't know me. He spoke to me and asked me if I had finished and I told him that I had. All the relevant measurements were obtained and the vehicle was loaded onto the recovery lorry. Everyone left the scene and the road was re-opened.

It is standard procedure in fatal road accidents for a Scenes of Crime Officer (SOCO) to attend to take photographs for evidential purposes for any prosecution and inquest. The following morning I received a phone call from the investigating officer informing me that the official SOCO photographer had attended the scene last night and was surprised to find that the scene had been cleared. The investigating officer had wrongly assumed that I was the SOCO photographer! With no shots of the scene, he wanted my photos. The fact that they were on transparencies did not matter. I later had to appear at the inquest with the photos as I was the first police officer on the scene. The final result was that the deceased driver was five times over the limit on blood alcohol. Accidental death was recorded by the coroner.

A Little Yellow Friend

One day I was officially on duty from 08:00 to 16:00. I had wanted to get off on time as it was my birthday and I was being taken out for a meal.

At 14:30 I popped into Saffron Walden Police Station to drop off some paperwork and have a cup of tea with the late turn shift, who I wanted to speak to about a job in Thaxted that I needed some assistance with. While we were drinking our tea, the Inspector came rushing in stating that a call had come in reporting a serious road accident in a nearby village. I shot out and the Inspector came with me.

We were soon at the scene and discovered carnage. A full minibus had gone through a wall and there were bodies everywhere. The fire brigade, ambulances and more police were soon on the scene. While I assisted the ambulance men, I suddenly found a yellow budgerigar sitting amongst the wreckage. I picked it up, it was happy to be handled, and gently placed it in my raincoat pocket. After all the casualties had been removed from the scene, I was redeployed to man one end of the road closure while traffic officers began to try and unravel what exactly had happened. By this time it was dark and I put my high visibility jacket on.

After about half an hour of waving my arms around, I suddenly felt a movement in my pocket and the budgie appeared and flew off into the night. I thought no more of it and continued directing the little traffic that was coming through. After another half an hour, the budgie reappeared and landed, to my utter surprise, at my feet and sat near my boot. I reached down, picked it up and placed it back in my pocket.

Much later I went off duty and back at my office I placed the bird, which seemed quite happy, into a cage before realising I had missed my birthday meal! I later gave the bird to a friend to look after and it transpired that a smashed up bird cage had been found in the crashed vehicle from the accident, which had been taken to HQ for examination.

Despite the trauma that the bird had undergone it survived and settled in to its new home.

A Dog With Attitude

Dogs have always been a problem for police officers, whether they are biting people, attacking livestock or just generally being out of control. The normal procedure when a dog attacks someone is that the dog had to be identified by the injured party, in front of the owner of the dog, who would then be reported for failing to keep the dog under control. This normally resulted in a court appearance (not by the dog but the owner) who would be ordered to keep the miscreant under control. If the dog breached the order the court could then order its destruction. As a Wildlife Officer most of these cases locally were passed on to me.

Thaxted had its fair share of dogs, the majority of which were fine, but there was always one. This particular yellow Labrador-type dog had a bad reputation. It was a particularly nasty individual and already had a court order on it to keep it under control. One morning I received a complaint from a local postman that he had been bitten by this dog. The dog was formally identified in front of the owner's wife and arrangements were made for me to see the owner that evening.

After dark the same day I went to the house; the dog was in the garden. As I stood at the gate the owner came to the front door and beckoned me in, stating that the dog was alright. He came out and grabbed the dog's collar and as I walked through the gate the dog dragged the owner over to me. I approached the front door with the man and the dog walking by my side. Suddenly, and without warning, the dog lunged at my leg and bit hard. Fortunately it bit my truncheon which was in a special pocket that ran down the inside of my trouser leg! The dog had locked on to my leg and was shaking it violently, ripping my trousers but not hurting me. The owner eventually managed to drag the dog off me and kept saying, "He's not dangerous really."

I was not happy - I declined a cup of tea and reported the owner, who I think sensed my unhappiness. A few days later the dog was put down by a vet. I do not like to see dogs put down, I currently have three Labradors of my own, but there comes a time when there is no other choice.

I had to request a new pair of uniform trousers and a new truncheon. The dog had almost bitten through my original one which was no mean feat. I hate to think what would have happened to my leg if the truncheon hadn't been there.

Missing Person(s)

In Thaxted there are two fairly large senior citizens residential establishments, and occasionally a resident would go out for a walk and forget how to get home. Eventually they would be reported missing to me and a search would be undertaken. Normally they were found within a short time and returned but occasionally they would simply disappear and the search would be scaled up with numerous police officers attending. The following are just a few of the more memorable ones from my long career at Thaxted.

One lady by the name Dot Hinds who was in her early 80s, began going missing on a fairly regular basis. She was a big woman and a very strong walker. She would arrive at the edge of the village and would then walk in a straight line, through fields and hedges. This habit usually meant that she was normally fairly easy to find by simply following her trail. But on one occasion I could not find her anywhere so the 'cavalry' were requested and within a short time my office was full. The search was being co-ordinated by the Duty Inspector from Saffron Walden, but it was left to me to deploy everyone. Soon teams were out all over Thaxted and the surrounding fields. After about four hours she still had not been found, so more and more officers were drafted in, this was before the days of the force helicopter.

The Duty Inspector had gone off across the fields behind the police office, heading in the general direction of Cutlers Green. I could see him striding out on the footpath and it was at that point that I realised that his radio wasn't working, as when I called him I got no reply.

By 18:00 the incident had been scaled up to a major incident and the Divisional Commander had been appraised and was en route from Harlow as Thaxted was within the Harlow Division. The Inspector had disappeared from view, so I sent a car around to Cutlers Green in an attempt to intercept him. They soon returned without him.

I sent two officers down to the church to see if by chance Dot was in there, but they radioed in to say that it was locked. I knew that there had been a wedding there earlier in the day and I rang the key holder to ask if he would attend the church and let the officers in. When they gained access, there was Dot, sitting near the altar, eating the communion wafers and totally oblivious to the mayhem outside. She was returned home.

However, we still could not find the Inspector so I did not want to stand anyone down until he was found. As the Divisional Commander arrived, the phone went in my office, it was the Inspector. On discovering that his radio wasn't working, he had called at a house between Cutlers Green and Debden Green and had used a phone. I advised him that Dot had been found alive and well and I sent a car to pick him up.

Everyone was stood down and I gave the Inspector and the boss a cup of tea and discussed Dot's disappearance. From that day the church was always one of the first places to be checked when a missing person was reported, and we checked that all the radios were working!

On another occasion, one mid-morning, an elderly lady, Hilda Cook who was a diabetic and registered blind, was reported missing. I made my usual search of the area with no trace. I was joined by other officers and a more thorough search was commenced. A witness had seen the lady walking up an alleyway leading to the school fairly early in the morning, so I concentrated the search in that area, including door-to-door enquiries, but had no luck.

By lunchtime the search had become a major operation and the Divisional Commander was sitting in my office coordinating the incident. More and more officers were drafted in to help, including the entire early turn shifts from Harlow and Chelmsford. We still did not have a force helicopter, but the boss managed to recruit an RAF helicopter from RAF Coltishall in Norfolk, which was airborne on a training exercise, and within thirty minutes it was hovering over Thaxted and the surrounding fields.

I was in the office running a log on the incident and making tea for the troops when the phone rang. It was a local resident who had been visited by an officer and after he had left, she had had a thought. Early that morning a coach trip had picked up a group of pensioners in a road near the school and had gone to Felixstowe for a day out. They were having lunch at a Royal British Legion Hall.

I made a few phone calls and a local officer in Felixstowe called at the hall. There, sitting with a group, was dear old Hilda, drinking tea and tucking into a cake, totally oblivious to the chaos she had caused in Thaxted. I informed the boss and everyone was stood down, including the helicopter. All were relieved that Hilda had been found alive and well, I had begun to fear the worst.

The next incident again involved an old lady resident of one of the homes, Elsie Parrish. She enjoyed a drink, so much so that she had a bar slate in a local pub! She really enjoyed her brandy and one particular night she consumed a considerable amount and left the pub at 21:30 as she had to be home by 22:00, she never arrived and at 23:00 she was reported missing to me. The home was searched with no trace. Along with a number of members of staff, we made a search of the town. I called at the pub where the licensee confirmed that she had been in as usual and left at her usual time.

The divisional control room was informed and officers were drafted in to assist in a search of the area. It was mid-winter and cold. By the early hours the search continued but I was advised to stand down, as I would be required at first light to coordinate the search.

I came back on duty at 06:00 and Elsie was still missing. Officers were being drafted in and the new force helicopter had been requested. We had a fairly sharp frost that night and I was very doubtful that she was still alive.

The helicopter soon arrived, landed on the recreation field and I briefed the crew. Within a short while of being airborne a call came in that they had found her in a ditch about a mile out of the town - she was alive. An ambulance was sent to the location and Elsie was checked over and appeared to be none the worse for her night out under the stars. Did the brandy keep her alive?

The final incident involving a missing person involved a trip in the helicopter for me! A young boy came home from school one evening and immediately had a row with his father, which resulted in him running away from the house on the outskirts of the town. His parents searched high and low for him with no trace and eventually attended my office to report him missing. By this time a good hour and a half had elapsed since he had last been seen. I contacted the control room, an incident was created and the troops mustered at my office.

All the lad's mates were checked but with no luck. The helicopter was already airborne returning to its base when the crew heard the incident on the police radio and a description of the boy being circulated. The crew offered their services and were dispatched to Thaxted, where they landed on the recreation ground. With my local knowledge I was taken up to try and coordinate the search.

It was not my first trip in a helicopter, but my first over Thaxted. As we lifted off the ground and into the clear blue evening sky the first thing that struck me was the number of swimming pools in the area. I know it sounds odd, but of course you can not see them on the ground. After checking the town area we drifted out to the fields and woods around the town.

As we moved towards the windmill I saw a courting couple in the tram lines of a tall crop of wheat - the partially clad couple were most embarrassed. The last thing they expected was a police helicopter hovering above them so we left them to their courting.

We lifted a little higher and hovered over a wood to the east of the town, near where the boy lived. It was interesting to see a male sparrowhawk fly out of the wood and speed away; it is not often that you can watch a beautiful hawk like this from above. We were high enough that there was no down draft from the rotas to affect the bird.

We continued our search of the outskirts and eventually I spotted a youth sitting in the middle of a wheat field, like the courting couple he was in the tram lines and totally concealed at ground level. He looked quite frightened as we hovered high above him so we moved away slightly while a car was sent to collect the boy, the crew of the car had quite a walk through the huge field to collect him. We hovered some way away just in case he ran off, but he didn't. He was returned home and I was dropped off at the recreation ground. I knew the boy and his parents quite well so I jumped into my police car and after standing everybody down I went to the house and had a chat with the boy. He was very upset, as were his parents; and very apologetic - he wouldn't do that again!

Goats

Just a short distance from my office was a pub known as the Fox and Hounds. In the mid 1980s a new licensee moved in and with him he brought two goats, a pure white one and a black and brown one. Both were females. He grazed the goats by tethering them on the pub lawn on chains.

The licensee did not last long and did what we term in the job as a 'runner', leaving a lot of unpaid bills and the two goats. Word reached me that the animals had been left without food or water and I contacted the local RSPCA Inspector; together we attended the premises. I was off duty at the time. Sure enough there were the two animals tethered to the lawn, which was pretty sparse as it was midsummer. There was no water placed out for them and when we offered them some it was apparent that they were really thirsty.

We stood and debated what was to be done with them before going back to my office where the Inspector made a few phone calls but had no luck in finding a place for them. At that time behind the new police house and office was about three acres of scrub that belonged to the Police Authority. It had formed the gardens of the two old police houses that were pulled down just after we moved into the new house and office. We took a walk out there and I offered to take the goats temporarily and tether them on this ground where I could keep an eye on them. The Inspector agreed and we led the goats on their chains down the road, with my Jack Russell terrier 'Cassie' following along at some distance behind - she was not too sure about these curious animals and they were not sure of her.

We pegged them down on the grass and they immediately tucked in to the abundant food supply. I rang a scrap dealer friend of mine and he brought over on his low loader, a scrapped small van with all the windows in and no wheels. I had it deposited on the grass behind my garage and scrounged some bales of straw from a local farmer for bedding inside the van. The seats had been removed before it was brought over.

The second day of the goats' stay I lost most of the cabbages that I was growing on a vegetable patch I had created behind the garage. The goats had managed to pull the pegs out and raided my vegetable patch!

After the incident in my vegetable patch the goats learnt a few ground rules and they soon settled into their new environment and the routine of being shut in the van at night and grazing during the day. However, there was one incident that occurred that I will never forget. It was a lovely sunny morning and I was sitting in the office completing some paperwork, a policeman's dread. I happened to look out onto the road as Cassie was sitting by the office door, which was glass. Suddenly she started barking excitedly. I then saw the cause of her excitement as the two goats went past the office door and along the drive to the road where they broke into a run, dragging their chains behind them with the pegs bouncing around on end.

I ran out and gave chase down the road but when the goats saw me they accelerated away, dodging in and out of the approaching traffic. Several drivers stopped and joined me on foot. We soon reached the Bull Ring corner and the church beyond. All the traffic had come to a halt, which was gratifying for our safety and that of the goats. At the church the goats were ushered into the church car park and the graveyard beyond.

At this point I was joined by two colleagues from Dunmow - someone had rung the police and suggested that I could do with some assistance! With the goats now settling down to graze in the churchyard, grabbing their chains was not difficult. I led one and a colleague led the other back up the road to the office and the goats' van, where I shut them in with some relief. I arranged with a local blacksmith for two long steel pins to be made and the goats did not escape again.

The temporary lodgings for the goats lasted for almost two years until I got news that developers were going to start building on the site that the goats now regarded as their home. I managed to find a goat rescue centre and eventually they were collected and soon settled down in their new home. I missed them for quite a while as I had grown attached to them. I had not experienced goats before and it was a steep learning curve. When you get to know and understand them they are quite endearing creatures, except when they were 'playing' with the cars - or eating my vegetables!

Wine Galore!

In the early 1980s, I got the bug for making home made wine and went into it in a big way. I made gallons of the stuff from rhubarb to orange and barley. The one gallon demijohns that stored the fermenting wine needed to be kept at room temperature and, of course, they took up a lot of space. The wine fermentation was started in the airing cupboard upstairs and then moved to the office. We had a dining table in the office and this was perfect. On some occasions there would be 20-30 demijohns bubbling away through the airlocks. My hobby attracted some interest from visitors to the office and colleagues.

One particular police visitor to my office was the Assistant Chief Constable (Operations)(ACC) who I knew as he had risen through the ranks. I offered him a cup of tea and we had a long chat. I answered the phone when it rang and it was the Chief Constable of Merseyside who wanted to speak to the ACC. After a brief chat he said, "You'll never believe this but I am sitting in one of my village beat offices and the wine is bubbling away," and he laughed. When he left I gave him a bottle to share with his wife. Much later I received a note through the internal mail, stating that he and his wife enjoyed the bottle of rhubarb wine very much.

After a couple of years of brewing I decided to enter some local competitions. The first was at Thaxted Gardeners' Show where there was a class for home made wine. I entered a bottle of elderberry, a bottle of rhubarb, and a bottle of orange and barley. I swept the board with 1st, 2nd and 3rd. After the show the judge wanted to buy a bottle, which of course would have been an offence without a licence so I gave him a bottle!

The second show was at a village fete in one of my villages. I placed three bottles into the home made wine class, a bottle of elderflower, a bottle of blackberry and a bottle of orange and barley, the latter was one of my favourites. There were quite a few entries, including some very obscure samples. The judge had been brought in from Cambridge and was a professional. I didn't get to the fete until quite late in the day as I had been on early shift. To my utter surprise I had swept the board again with a 1st, 2nd and 3rd. The same woman had won the wine class for a number of years and had expected to do so again this year. Her nose had been put right out of joint, and she made a very sarcastic comment to me as I collected my rosettes and cup. She was a local magistrate and chair of the local parish council - not a lady to upset - she did not speak to me for months! The silence was finally broken when I brought a local poacher before her at the local Magistrates Court. Discretion being the better part of valour, I decided not to put an entry in this village fete again.

Public Order Training

Whilst still at Ongar, I had been to a number of public order situations, with very little training. Incidents such as a riot at Essex University and a dock workers dispute at Harwich. Soon after arriving at Thaxted, I was one of a number of rural officers that underwent a period of intensive training for public order situations.

Most of the training was at Wethersfield Air Base near Braintree, which in those days was occupied by a US Air Force Squadron. The training involved rapid debussing and forming cordons, trudging and wedging, which basically meant forming a block of officers to move forward en mass to break up groups of demonstrators who, for the training, were cadets from the police training school. From there we went on to the recently introduced plastic shields, the original ones being 6ft tall. We held them in line as wooden bricks were thrown at us - they certainly hurt if they hit you so you soon learnt to miss them. It was disconcerting to see the bricks hurtling towards you and it was difficult not to flinch. In later years' training, the wooden bricks were replaced with real bricks and iron bars, bottles, and finally the ultimate, petrol bombs!

One memorable incident, involved a support unit call to Brighton. Sussex Police had requested assistance from a number of regional forces for the closure of the Conservative Party Conference, by the Prime Minister, Margaret Thatcher. There was a march by 15,000+ people, campaigning for the right to work, amongst other things. Essex sent 100 officers in a convoy of police personnel carriers.

The rendezvous was at Police HQ at Chelmsford at 04:00 and the convoy left for the sunny beaches of Brighton, the only trouble was that it rained heavily all day. The convoy looked quite impressive as we travelled along the motorway, but much bigger ones were to be experienced during the miners' strike in 1984.

We were deployed along the seafront in front of the conference centre, which was all glass. The beach below us was all pebbles - not a good combination - and had been declared a 'No Go' area for the public. We were standing in a long line getting soaked when I happened to look down on to the beach in time to see a rather amusing incident. A little old lady had managed to evade the cordon preventing people from going onto the beach. She was walking her little Yorkshire Terrier on a lead. Suddenly two huge Hampshire police officers walked across the beach to the old lady, who appeared tiny against them. They spoke to her but it was obvious from the body language that she was ignoring them.

Suddenly, with very little effort, the officers who were standing either side of her lifted her up gently between them and walked her off the beach, with her little legs swinging out between the two giants and the dog running along behind. She was brought up the steps to where we were standing and then released. She scuttled off shouting something uncomplimentary about the police and the

Conservatives, the confused dog was scuttling along behind.

Soon after that incident we were redeployed to disperse a large, angry crowd that had formed near the Conference Centre. We formed a 'wedge' that was six officers deep at the widest point. I was toward the front - not a good place to be. As we approached the crowd a number of missiles came raining in, thank goodness for our helmets (this was a few years before full riot equipment was deployed by the

police). Now, bear in mind that we were soaking wet, the rain was dripping off our helmets, flour bombs began to rain in on us from the crowd so the order came from the Inspector at the back of the wedge to speed up, which we did. I had received two direct flour bomb hits, one to my helmet and one to the front of my raincoat - flour and water mix very well! The crowd dispersed before we reached them and no one was arrested. Looking around at my colleagues we did look a motley crowd, the officers at the front had taken the full force of the bombs.

We went back to the rendezvous point to try and clean up but it was a waste of time. We were sent back to our previous point on the sea front where we remained for the rest of the duty. It was a long day, we were eventually released by Sussex Police at 20:00 and began to make our way home, but that was not the end of the day.

As we were leaving Brighton on a dual carriageway section (I was driving) there was a small saloon car ahead of us with a police carrier ahead of it and another two in the outside lane. For some reason, known only to the Sergeant sitting next to me in the front, he decided to check the vehicle on the police National Computer (PNC) and lo and behold it came up as a vehicle stolen from Brighton about an hour beforehand. We could see that there were two people in the car and the other police vehicles had heard the report. As we had him well and truly penned in we all put on our blue lights and slowed down to a stop. The occupants of the stolen car decided to try and run away from the car, the wrong decision as 30 huge officers, many of whom were rugby players, descended on the hapless pair who became buried under a scrum, or was it a ruck? It just wasn't their day!

The Miners' Strike

In 1984 the country saw one of the biggest industrial disputes ever seen when the National Union of Miners (NUM), with their leader Arthur Scargill, took on the

Conservative government under Margaret Thatcher, primarily over proposed pit closures. The dispute turned into one of the longest, most bitter and most expensive in history.

Policing the dispute involved officers from virtually every force in the country and I had my fair share with twelve weeks on the dispute, stretching from the very beginning of the dispute to the very end after almost fourteen months. Most of my time was spent in Nottinghamshire, Leicestershire and South Yorkshire. I had had no experience of the mining industry prior to this dispute; it was an experience that I would never forget.

My first week of action was the second week of the dispute and the police operational machine was still grinding into gear. The instruction was that the Essex contingent of over 300 officers would rendezvous at Police HQ, which was a logistical nightmare. The convoy that left Essex was nearly a mile long, with police personnel carriers, each containing a crew of ten including a Sergeant. Support vehicles were also in the convoy, including motorcycle outriders that would ride on ahead and seal off roundabouts and traffic lights to enable us to have a free, uninterrupted passage through built up areas. The convoy looked very impressive and, in a way, rather frightening - what was the country coming to? It felt a little like George Orwell.

Our normal route was via the A1 to the north. After three hours on the road we arrived at our billet, which was an army training camp known as 'Proteus'.

The camp looked very impressive as a film of World War Two had just been made there and it had been transformed into a prison camp with barbed wire everywhere and wooden guards' towers strategically placed all around. The accommodation consisted of the long wooden huts used in the filming. Each hut would contain about 20 officers, and there was a large wood burning stove in the middle, with the chimney going up and out through the roof. We soon learnt that these stoves would burn anything! The huts were quite cold but after the first couple of days, we were so tired that we would sleep anywhere.

Our first responsibility was a pit called Bilsthorpe where coal was mined and processed. This involved crushing the coal into powder for injecting into the burners for an electricity power station. The miners at this pit had decided to break the strike and continue working. This had obviously angered the NUM and so the striking miners, called 'Flying Pickets', were deployed by the Union to stop them working in any way they could. Our role was to keep the two factions apart to prevent a breach of the peace. Our first week was fairly quiet and I spent most of the days walking around the village of Bilsthorpe, as miners' houses and cars had also been targeted in an attempt to intimidate the miners - I don't think that I have ever drunk so much tea! We returned home on the Friday night, not in convoy, and after we were dropped off the vehicles were taken to HQ for service, ready for the next crew on Sunday.

My next visit was about four weeks later, but this time I was Acting Sergeant, a role I had been regularly undertaking over a period of time. We were back at Proteus and nothing had changed apart from the catering arrangements, which had luckily improved! We were still at Bilsthorpe as the pit continued to operate despite being hit by gangs of pickets. Even one of the long rubber conveyor belts carrying the coal had been slashed at the bottom of a 1600' mine shaft – goodness knows how. We were again lucky with a relatively quiet week. We were on the early shift and this meant that we started at 04:00 at the pit, which was quite a way from Proteus. On the Thursday we received an invitation from the pit manager to go down and visit the pit face. It was cleared by our Duty Inspector on the understanding that he could come with us. I had some reservations, as I do sometimes suffer with claustrophobia, but I knew that it was either we all go or not at all, and I didn't want to be the odd one out. As soon as our relief had arrived we were all togged up in boiler suits, miners' helmets and lamps. We were also given two tags, one to be handed in to the lift man on going down and one to be handed in on our return.

The trip down was, to say the least, interesting. Once we were all in and had our lamps switched on, the miner taking us down warned us about the acceleration of the lift, but nothing could have prepared us for the feeling when the lift started and dropped at 16' per second - our stomachs were on the roof of the cage. Almost halfway down the lift stopped as sharply as it had started; two or three of us picked ourselves up from the floor! The miner then asked us all to switch off our lamps and we were plunged into total darkness. It was a darkness that I had never experienced before and it was quite a relief when we turned our lamps back on.

At the bottom we came to an abrupt stop, I'm sure the miner was having some fun with us. My knees were really aching. We stepped out into a small enclosed area and a big metal door was closed behind us, after which a similar door on the opposite side was opened and we all stepped out - this was a form of air lock. I will always remember that the first thing that struck me was the wind, I had never considered that ventilation was needed underground. The floor was covered in a thick, white dust which was antiblast powder. This blew up onto our clothing all the time we were down there. We were shown around and the process of actually mining the coal was explained; we then moved off along a tunnel. I was very conscious of all that rock above us but tried to dismiss it from my mind, not an easy task. We were approaching a lot of noise and eventually came out into another tunnel where a huge belt was racing past us carrying the coal - this was the source of the noise.

We walked along a path with the belt racing past us. The miner explained that we would not be walking to the current work face as it was two miles away, however, we did walk quite a long way in partial darkness with our lamps on before turning off and entering a dark tunnel, which was only illuminated by our lamps. We walked a long way along this tunnel until we suddenly, and unexpectedly, came upon a wall of coal - this had been the old coal face many years ago but as the coal seam began to run out a new one was commenced. We were then all given the opportunity to 'mine' a piece of coal for ourselves. The miner then went into some detail as to how the coal was formed and how it was extracted. It was really fascinating.

After almost two hours underground we returned to the surface and I for one was exhausted. The whole experience had been fantastic and was an opportunity of a lifetime, one that I will never ever forget, particularly overcoming my phobia. I am very, very proud of the piece of coal that I mined and have it on display in a cabinet in my office.

Another pit that we were based at was called Treeton Colliery. We were again taken underground but this time we were in an open train from the surface, which then went into a tunnel. It then began to drop in stages, which was very disorientating in the dark as the angle of descent became more and more acute. It was like a roller coaster. Down and down we went, and faster and faster we appeared to be going. We travelled for what seemed an age - I for one did not like it. We suddenly came to a fairly abrupt halt.

We got off with our helmet lamps lit and walked a short distance to another train. We then travelled for what seemed like another age but apparently was about 45 minutes on the flat, the noise from this train was quite deafening. From there we walked a few hundred yards to a face where the miner leading the group gave us a talk above all the noise and, like Bilsthorpe, the tremendous breeze. His opening comment was unforgettable, "We are now approximately thirty miles under the north sea." We all looked at each other in disbelief and with some trepidation. After another two hours underground we boarded the second train to the surface, I was quite relieved to see daylight again.

As far as the catering went, after a few weeks Nottingham Police had got it about right. Whichever shift we were on, we were provided with a packed lunch in a brown paper bag. This contained a sandwich, a meat pie in a silver dish, a piece of fruit (normally an apple), a packet of crisps and a drink.

One week I was acting Sergeant on a carrier that had been deployed on a huge roundabout on the A1 at Grantham, on the edge of Sherwood Forest - we were on the look out for flying pickets. During the week we had our usual packed lunches and midweek one of the crew suggested that we heated the pies up on the transit's engine, so we very carefully placed all ten of the pies inside the engine, mostly on the radiator, then shut the bonnet down.

A few minutes later we got a shout over the radio to assist another Essex unit a short distance away, who had stopped a coach load of pickets and the situation was getting out of hand.

Forgetting about the pies we shot off to assist. We had only travelled a short distance when there was an awful sound of crunching coming from the engine. A horrible smell seeped into the transit along with smoke. We arrived at the scene fairly quickly and everyone piled out coughing and spluttering. Fortunately the coach had been turned around and was being escorted out of the county. Smoke was billowing out from under the bonnet as I carefully opened it. The sight that greeted me was incredible. The underside of the bonnet was splattered all over with pieces of meat and gravy. The engine was unrecognisable, with shreds of silver all over the place and the entire engine was covered in meat and gravy, which was gently cooking. We cleaned off what we could before driving to a garage to refuel and, with a power washer, cleaned off more of the mess but there was still a lot within the engine compartment. The smell remained with us for the rest of the week and when the vehicle was left at our HQ on the Friday for service, we left a note saying that a rabbit had gone up into the engine. One of my mates that worked in the garage sent me a note through the internal mail asking if the Nottinghamshire rabbits come wrapped in silver foil!

A few weeks after that incident, I was back up in Nottingham and on the A1 roundabout again. One of the lads on our carrier had brought up a miniature barbeque with all the trimmings. On the Monday morning on our way to our point, we stopped off at a supermarket and bought a load of meat: sausages, beef burgers and pork chops. We set up the cooker behind the carrier out of sight of prying eyes and ate very well that week.

On the Thursday of that week the barbeque was going flat out - as it was our last day we had treated ourselves to steaks amongst other things – and there was a lot of smoke billowing out from behind the carrier. We always maintained two officers standing on the roundabout close to the carrier, these acted as spotters, that was all that was needed at any one time and they were relieved on the hour. The rest of us were either in or around the carrier.

As we tucked into our steaks a big chauffeur-driven car rolled up and stopped in front of us and I saw a police officer get out of the back and put his hat on. I immediately recognised him as the Deputy Chief Constable of Essex, who was the senior officer in charge of the operation in Nottingham for that week. We continued eating, but stood up as he reached us; he jovially told us to continue eating. We offered him some food which he accepted. He beckoned his chauffeur to join us and they both tucked in to a hearty lunch washed down with a nice cup of tea, the water having been boiled on the barbeque. He sat and talked to us for quite a while before thanking us for lunch and leaving. Our cooking exploits became quite a talking point. A few years later he came out to visit me at Thaxted and we spoke about the miners' strike, he never forgot the barbeque. He said, "Only the Essex officers would have the ingenuity to do something like that", he did enjoy it!

One final amusing incident involved an urn that we 'acquired' one week when I was up at Proteus, again as Acting Sergeant for the week. This was a week when we saw quite a lot of action. We were not attached to a particular pit but were backing up any units that had trouble. One of the lads on our carrier was Micky Page or 'Bungalow' - how he got that nickname I do not know. Like me he was a village bobby, at Leaden Roding near Dunmow, and like me he was on the dispute on odd weeks when numbers were short.

Now Mick claimed to have a way with electrics and told me that he could wire up the urn to the lighter socket on our transit. I knew very little about electrics, so I left it to him. We arrived at one pit where trouble had broken out and, having sorted it out, Mick decided to boil up some water. He put the wires of the urn lead into the lighter socket and we sat and waited. Suddenly I saw smoke coming out from under the dashboard and pulled the wires out in a hurry. Fortunately no long term damage was caused and we returned the urn to the Metropolitan Police hut from where we had 'borrowed' it.

The dispute was not confined to the Midlands and the North but had also spread to the Essex ports of Brightlingsea and Wivenhoe where coal was being brought in on ships. Early one morning I was part of a crew on a carrier that had been deployed to Brightlingsea. A ship carrying coal was to be unloaded into lorries and trouble was expected. A fleet of coaches with flying pickets from Kent were en route to the port. We were part of a large contingent of Essex officers deployed to the port.

On our arrival we were met by a barrage of abuse. We were called 'Thatcher's Thugs'; it was very noisy and chaotic. A lot of people were sitting down in the road, effectively blocking the roads to the lorries. We received the call to go in and clear the road and all went in to drag everyone away. I dragged one or two away but they immediately returned and sat down. One old lady that I dragged to the path immediately returned to the road and sat down right in front of me. I had already warned her that she was leaving herself open to being arrested for breaching the peace. She refused to move or cooperate so I arrested her and, with assistance from a colleague, she was dragged kicking and screaming to the carrier. I was a little taken aback by the struggle she put up; I did not think she had it in her.

In the carrier she calmed down and told me that she was 83 years old. She turned out to be a lovely old girl and we got on like a house on fire; she was later released without charge. A few months later, after the miners' strike had finished I met her again at a cubbing hunt meet at the beginning of the hunting season, at Great Canfield near Dunmow. She was holding a placard, all credit to her. I did not arrest her this time, as she behaved herself!

I had a total of twelve weeks on the dispute and have very many fond memories of which these are but a few. Although these are amusing memories, there were many flash points that turned very ugly. The hours were long and tiring and, of course, we were away from our families for weeks at a time. Many of us thought that this dispute might bring the prospect of a National Police Force that much closer, but at the time of writing this book, some 22 years later, it still seems a far off prospect.

Police Surgeries

After the miners' strike I made every effort to get back into the communities that I was responsible for. In an attempt to achieve this I was given approval to conduct police 'surgeries' in two of the more remote villages by using their village halls for two hours every month. I would sit in the halls and make myself available to the local residents. I could answer any queries they might have, deal with complaints, give information, or would just have a chat. They were launched with a blaze of publicity and became very popular.

The dates of the surgeries were advertised locally and I had a regular stream of visitors at every one. I was obtaining statements and conducting other enquiries at the surgeries and a lot of information came flowing in. The information ranged from who was responsible for a spate of local fly-tipping incidents, which led to a successful prosecution, to who was having an affair with whom, and other local gossip. It is always useful for a local officer to know what is happening on his or her beat.

One dear old lady, Elsie Turner, who lived near the village hall at Hempstead, would call into every surgery with a mug of tea and a piece of Dundee cake wrapped in newspaper. She was very lonely and would sit and talk to me throughout the surgery, even if other people came in to see me, and over time we became good friends. One evening I was in the village hall as usual when she came in with my tea and two packages of newspaper. She placed them on my table and one went down fairly heavily onto the wood – was it a rock cake? As she sat down I opened the first package and there was my slice of cake. I then opened the second package, which seemed quite heavy. Elsie was unusually quiet and I was soon to discover why. As the paper came apart, there before me was a 'pineapple' hand grenade! It was pristine; it was so clean it virtually gleamed. Rather startled, I immediately checked to see if the pin was in, which thankfully it was!

I looked somewhat surprised at Elsie, who didn't say a word to begin with. I turned to her and asked her where it had come from. She became very upset and started crying. I comforted her as she told me the story of the grenade. Her husband Bill had brought it home from the war along with a load of bits and pieces which were placed in a tea chest in their loft. Bill had passed away two years before and their son had been sorting through some items in the loft when he came upon the chest and found the very dirty, dusty grenade. He told his mother to hand it in to me at the next surgery.

It had played on her mind so much that she had decided to bury it in her garden, which she did. It remained there for a week, but she was not happy about it being there so she dug it up. I asked her how it had come to be so clean and she told me that she had washed it and cleaned it with a wire brush! I took it back to the office and immediately rang the Bomb Disposal Team who came out and collected it. They did state that it was live and that it was the cleanest one they had ever seen - I did not tell them how that came about. Elsie was very grateful to me for disposing of it for her and we did laugh about it at the following surgery.

Another memorable incident at one of the surgeries involved the press and a prisoner. It was a lovely summer evening and I was sitting in Great Sampford village hall near the open front door to take advantage of a gentle breeze. I was just enjoying a cup of tea that an old boy from the house opposite had brought over when a car pulled up outside the hall. A gentleman got out and I immediately recognised him as a local press photographer. He came in and told me that one of the local papers was running a feature about my surgeries and he had been sent to get some shots of me.

He had taken one or two shots of me sitting at the table when a very dishevelled, unshaven, scruffy middle-aged man, who I did not recognise, walked into the hall. He was covered in mud and had dried grass in his hair. He walked up to my table and said, "I think you want me." He had a broad Scottish accent. I asked, "Why is that?" He said, "I've screwed a few houses here and the police in Edinburgh want me." The reporter was listening intently as I asked the man to sit down. I took down his details - his name was Jim MacDonald and it turned out that he had been sleeping rough for the past few days. He admitted to me that he had burgled a few isolated properties in the area over the past few days, mainly for food and cash and I arrested him straight away.

I radioed his details through to my control and a few checks on Jim revealed that he was wanted in Edinburgh for a large number of dwelling burglaries and a number of other forces also wanted to speak to him. The reporter asked me to step outside and then asked if he could use this story in the paper. I suggested that he should speak to the Inspector at Saffron Walden. He wanted to photograph Jim but I refused.

I took Jim into Saffron Walden Police Station where I interviewed him with CID and he admitted to a lot more burglaries in our area. My boss was very pleased - the fact that Jim had given himself up was forgotten! The following week the press made a big feature about my surgeries and Jim's arrest, though he was not named. I believe that the final tally of burglaries and thefts that Jim admitted to throughout the Home Counties and Scotland was over 100. He was later convicted and sent down to do some time in the 'Queen's Hotel'.

The Metal Detector And The Missile

One bright, sunny morning I was on duty out on patrol, with Cassie for my Jack Russell terrier company, when I received a call on the radio asking me to return to my office. As I turned into the back yard of my office I spotted a large cylindrical object standing on the brick wall and leaning to one side. It had the appearance of a huge bullet. I went indoors, followed by Cassie, and spoke to my wife. She told me that a local metal detector operator had called at the police house carrying the object, which he said he had found in a field near Thaxted. She told him to place it around the back of the house. She actually meant on the waste ground behind the office, but he had placed it on the wall!

I examined the object and it appeared to be live. It was standing on what looked like its firing pin, which protruded out at the end causing the whole thing to lean. I very carefully lifted the object up and moved it out onto the waste ground before very gently laying it down in the grass. I rang the Bomb Disposal Team and described the object to them. They asked me where it was and when I told them that it had been brought to the office - they informed me that under no circumstances should it be moved!

Within two hours a Bomb Disposal Team had arrived. The object, which turned out to be a World War II armour-piercing shell, was very carefully carried out into a ploughed field next to the office and buried in a 4ft deep hole with a charge placed around it. A cable was led from it to the road, some 100ft from it. I tried ringing the farmer but there was no reply.

I had been joined by a colleague, as I had been asked to close the road temporarily while they blew the object up. At the allotted time the traffic was stopped and after a count of three there was a huge explosion in the field and a column of soil rose high into the sky before raining down onto the road, me and the assembled audience. The explosion left a large crater in the field that took a little explaining to the farmer who, fortunately, was a friend of mine. The local media had a field day with the metal detector operator and praised him for bringing the object into the police - I did not fully share their sentiment. I did later suggest to him that if he found any more that he might leave them where they were and call us … immediately!

An Unusual Arrest!

As a village bobby I was expected to visit the licensed premises on my beat on a fairly regular basis, at least once a month. The visits were recorded and the records were inspected regularly by my senior officers. Generally I had a good working relationship with all the licensees as my wife and I would often pop into a local pub for a drink and a meal when I had some time off.

One particular premises was The Swan Hotel in Thaxted, opposite the church. The licensee was Frank White and over the years we became good friends; I would often call in there after going off duty for a swift half and a chat once everyone had left (I had a jacket over my uniform.)

One memorable evening, having had the day off, I had called into The Swan during the evening for a drink and a chat at closing time. Frank offered me a meal as he was about to eat as well. My wife was away in Canada at the time so this seemed a good opportunity to have a hot meal - I am not renowned for my cooking ability. Frank and I sat and chatted as we ate; we were the only people in the premises.

As we sat enjoying a nightcap after the meal, I suddenly heard the screech of tyres in the rear car park and almost immediately there was a loud banging on the back door. Frank went off to investigate and I heard a voice I recognised as David Wilson. David was a local lad who had been in a lot of trouble over the years for everything from car thefts to burglary. He shouted to Frank, "Get me away, the police are after me. Please Frank, hide me." He barged past Frank and ran around into the bar area where he caught sight of me. The expression on his face was priceless, as his bottom jaw dropped to the floor and he said, "Oh ...."

Frank, who had followed him through, was in hysterics. I sat David down and said to him, "What have you done this time David?" He then admitted that the car he had abandoned in the car park was stolen from Saffron Walden, and that the police were chasing him. Even David saw the funny side of the situation, as I rang the police after I had arrested him. While we waited for cavalry David said to me,

"How come you are everywhere Barry?" With tongue in cheek I replied, "That's my job David." I took him to Saffron Walden where he was later charged. The custody Sergeant couldn't really understand how I managed to make the arrest so late at night when I was off duty!

Lights, Camera, Action.

An amusing incident involving a shoplifting offence came in one Saturday morning, when I received a call from a local shop proprietor reporting three youths being filmed on a security camera in the shop whilst shoplifting at his premises.

I attended and viewed the film with the proprietor. It started with David and Chris Wilson and one other Thaxted youth entering the shop and walking up to one of the cameras. Although there was no sound, one could read Chris's lips, "Move the camera, move the camera." David moved forward, looked up at the camera, and his arm disappeared out of view under the camera which suddenly swung around on to another aisle. At this point the shop owner told me that he had suspected that they were up to no good and had asked a member of staff to watch them. She saw them move the camera and then take a quantity of car parts off the shelf and leave by a back door without paying.

The member of staff returned the camera to its original position just before the three came back into the shop and back to the aisle where they had stolen the spares. They started stealing more items without checking the camera.

Suddenly David looked up at the camera, said something and the other two stood up and looked straight at the camera - the look on their faces was priceless. The expression 'Gotcha' comes to mind. I arrested all three later that day and recovered all the stolen property. At the subsequent appearance at the Magistrates Court the film was shown to the justices who could not resist a wry smile. They meted out substantial fines.

A UFO

I have always been very sceptical about Unidentified Flying Objects (UFO) and have generally felt that there are always plausible explanations for these occurrences. However, my scepticism took a real knock about 25 years ago when I saw something that I still cannot explain.

I was on duty one cold, still, clear winter's evening. The dark night sky was full of bright stars. I was driving my police Mini van along the B1051 Sampford road back towards Thaxted. I looked over towards the south and the town and saw a very bright light in the sky. It appeared to be above a row of houses known as Wainsfield Villas. I didn't take much notice of it, assuming that it was an aircraft from Stansted airport, some nine miles away. However, as I watched I realised that the light was not moving and in fact it was too bright to be an aircraft.

I stopped the vehicle and got out. I had thought it might be a reflection within the vehicle but it wasn't. I had not got my binoculars with me as there was little point at night. I watched the light for about ten minutes and it didn't move or alter in its brilliance. I called up on the radio to ask control if they could contact Air Traffic Control at the airport to ascertain if they had any aircraft in the air in my vicinity. I explained why, which raised some curiosity at my control room, but the reply was in the negative. The airport, which at that time had not been developed, had very few night flights and nothing was showing on their radar. I was now getting very curious as I stood and watched it for another few minutes.

I eventually decided to drive around to the villas, trying to watch it as long as I could, but as I passed through the main street I lost sight of it. When I reached the villas I went to the point where I had calculated the light to be but there was nothing except for a very strange, tiny cloud just hanging over the road - there was no light emanating from it. There was still no breeze and the cloud was completely stationary.

Just as I was going to try and investigate further I was sent to investigate an alarm activation. On my way home I checked if the cloud was still there but it was nowhere to be seen and the night sky was clear again. I returned to the spot where I had first seen the light and there was no sign of it so I went home.

I kept quiet about it, but the following morning the local news was dominated by reports of strange, unexplained, bright lights all over East Anglia. I kept quiet about my experience for fear of ridicule by my colleagues; in fact this is the first time that I have mentioned it to anyone. When I initially called it in to control an incident was not created, fortunately!

What it was I will never know, but it was certainly quite spooky.

A Missing Person With A Difference

Christmas is often a busy time for the police, with the increased traffic more road accidents occur. In addition to this sudden deaths often increase over the festive period. A sudden death is one where the certifying doctor cannot give the cause of death and the coroner has to be informed; this is where the police come in. Violent and unexplained deaths also fall into this category.

Christmas is a time when many people overindulge and, tragically, this can sometimes result in death. As the local police officer I was expected to deal with these incidents as and when they occurred if I was on duty, which I normally was at some stage over the festive season.

One Boxing Day during a particularly cold snap of weather, the inevitable happened. I was called out to a sudden death in Thaxted by a local doctor. An elderly man, Bill Clarke, had been found dead in his flat by his daughter. Bill had not been seen by a doctor for some time and the doctor was left with no choice but to ring the police.

After the body had been formally identified by Bill's daughter, and the necessary paperwork had been completed, I arranged for a local undertaker to convey him and the paperwork to the Herts and Essex Hospital at Bishops Stortford, which in those days was our local hospital. My immediate responsibilities now finished, I had a cup of tea with Bill's daughter and then left - job done, or so I thought.

The following morning I was off duty when a knock came at the office door. I went through to the office and opened the door to find Bill's daughter and her husband standing outside. They asked if they could have a chat and I let them in. They opened the conversation by thanking me for all the work I did yesterday, then Bill's daughter said, "Can you tell me where Bill has gone?" The question surprised me a little as I had told them yesterday where her father's body was going. I said, "He has gone to the Herts and Essex Hospital." She replied, "That's what we thought, but he is not there." I was rather taken aback by this. I rang the undertaker who confirmed that the body had been left at the hospital as arranged. I then rang the hospital and spoke to the mortuary reception who confirmed that Bill's remains were not there. I was getting some anxious looks from the two behind the counter so I asked them to go home and I would sort it out. I assured them as they left that I would find out what had happened and where Bill's body was.

I rang the hospital again and explained the situation. I asked them to check their records once more as there must be some mistake. They advised me that they were full, as there had been a large number of sudden deaths due to the cold weather, and this was compounded by the fact that mortuary staff nationally were taking industrial action over a pay dispute; they said that they would ring me back. True to their word a few minutes later they rang back to say that as they were full, they had arranged for the body to be taken to Princess Alexandra's Hospital at Harlow; I felt a sense of relief.

I rang the Harlow hospital only to be advised that they were also full and Bill's body wasn't there - they did not know where he was. A wave of panic swept over me, how was I going to explain this to my boss? I asked them to double check but the result was the same. I had no option but to inform the duty Inspector who was not amused. His helpful comment to me was, "Only you could lose a body, Barry." He suggested that I started to ring around all the London hospitals and to keep a log of all my enquiries, the latter I was already doing.

I spent the next two hours ringing around virtually every hospital in the south east but still no luck, Bill had disappeared into thin air. I was amazed just how many sudden deaths had occurred over this Christmas period. After exhausting all the London hospitals I then turned my attention to hospitals in the neighbouring counties to the north of Essex. Late in the afternoon, I finally struck lucky. Bill had turned up at the West Suffolk Hospital at Bury St. Edmunds. I thanked them profusely but my relief turned to curiosity when the mortuary staff advised me that he had only just arrived - where had he been all this time? I was so relieved to have found him that I did not pursue that line of enquiry! I immediately informed his daughter who, luckily, thought the entire fiasco quite amusing - I didn't.

She came up to see me later in the week to inform me that the result of the post mortem had shown that Bill had died of a massive heart attack and the coroner was satisfied, therefore no inquest was required. She thanked me for all that I had done and as she left she said, "Do you know Barry, Dad travelled further in death than he ever did when he was alive?" Little did she know exactly how far he had travelled!

A Christmas Bird!

One Christmas Eve I was on duty in my office when the phone rang. It was my control at HQ, requesting that I attend a road accident on the road between Elsenham and Thaxted - other details were a bit vague. I jumped in the police car with Cassie and off we went. A few minutes later we were at the scene where a badly smashed up car was on the road. As I got out I was curious as to what the car had hit.

I spoke to the driver, a man in his mid 40s, who came out with the most surprising explanation, "Officer, you are not going to believe this, but I have just hit an ostrich!" I looked at him with some suspicion and said, "Have you been drinking, Sir?" He laughed and said, "I knew you were going to ask me that, and no I haven't." He provided a negative breath test.

A few yards into a field near the scene I found a dead ostrich - I could not believe my eyes. It was a huge bird - one of its legs alone was bigger than my Christmas turkey. When I contacted my control and advised them what we had they asked me if I had been drinking!

I completed all the necessary paperwork and arranged recovery of the vehicle, which was not driveable. I bagged up the corpse and took it back to my office where it was later collected by a farmer who had an ostrich farm at Henham. The amusing thing was that the gentleman was not legally required to report the accident as an ostrich is not an animal as defined under the road traffic act. An animal in this case is a horse, cattle, ass, mule, sheep, pig, goat or dog. When the paperwork reached HQ it caused a few hiccups!

In case you are wondering, we did not have the bird for Christmas dinner!

Morris Dancing

Soon after moving to Thaxted I was to learn that Morris Dancing was very popular in the town. On the first full weekend in June, every year for over 70 years, there was a big gathering of dancers with teams from all over the country and from overseas, and the weekend was known as the 'Ring' meeting. Over 300 dancers would descend on Thaxted on the Friday evening and dance on various pub forecourts until a late hour. My task with Dave Kinnley, the Thaxted special officer, was to make sure that the pubs cleared on time and with no trouble. If there were any problems it was usually from people not connected to the Morris ring, but outsiders coming in to take advantage of the extended licensing hours - this was a long time before all day licensing.

On the Saturday morning the teams would leave Thaxted at 09:00 on coaches and visit various locations in Suffolk, Cambridgeshire, Hertfordshire and Essex. As soon as they left I would put out in excess of 300 'Police No Waiting' cones, ably assisted by my son Phil, my daughter Georgina, and my late nephew Marc, along with all their mates - it certainly made my life easier. The purpose of the cones was to keep the main routes and the diversion open, as parking this weekend was often a problem for me.

Several thousand people have been known to descend on the town for the massed dancing, which is a very colourful spectacle.

Mid-afternoon on Saturday the coaches would slowly return to Thaxted and at 18:00, from either end of the town, two processions would dance down into the main street known as Town Street, where they would meet up. They would then dance either as individual teams or as a mass dance through the evening, with the final dance being performed by the Thaxted Morris Men. This dance was known as the 'Abbots Bromley Horn Dance'. It is an interesting dance with a lone fiddle playing as the men perform the dance. The audience are lulled into complete silence and you could hear a pin drop. I believe that Thaxted are the only team within the ring that are allowed to perform this dance.

When I first came to Thaxted traffic was allowed to pass through the dancing but this was extremely dangerous so David and I came up with a plan to divert traffic away from Town Street during the dancing. It was a tense moment for us when we implemented the diversion for the first time in 1978, but it worked, for light traffic anyway. Any HGVs, buses etc had to pass through the dancing, usually under escort by the Morris Fools, who normally extracted a 'donation' from the driver as money was collected over the weekend.

My task during the dancing was to walk along the edges ensuring that the audience kept back on the footpath. Numerous amusing incidents happened to Dave and I over the years. With my helmet on I was always a target for the fools. The Thaxted fool was a white horse with green markings known as Stilton, the dancer inside was a good friend, Peter Lawrence, whose children I had taught to ride their bikes under the Cycle Proficiency Scheme that I taught at a number of local schools.

On one occasion I was standing at one end of the street with the dancers in front of me. I did not see Stilton creeping up behind me, but the audience had. Suddenly my helmet rose off my head and Stilton ran off through all the dancers with it in his mouth - I was not going to give him the satisfaction of chasing him. One of the dancers took the helmet out of his mouth and put it firmly on Stilton's head. Eventually he walked back to me and bowed in front of me. I bowed back and as I went down I retrieved my helmet, the audience clapped as I pretended to kick Stilton in the rear as he ran off.

Another time we had a group of clog dancers from Lancashire. They were all huge men, both in girth and height. When it came to their individual dance they proceeded out of the crowd and the lead man grabbed my arm and dragged me into the middle of the street. They then danced around me, using me as a central point. I had no choice but to stand there until their dance had finished. Their fool, a dragon, came up to me and bowed. I bowed back and there was a lot of laughing and clapping as we all left the 'arena'.

On the Sunday of Morris Weekend, a number of teams would dance at lunch time outside the church, which happened to be opposite The Swan Hotel. Traffic control was required when they did mass dances, with the public performing traditional country dances. One year I had assistance from a female colleague from Saffron Walden. She got roped in to take part in one of the country dances and was happy to enter into the spirit of the moment. I had my camera nearby and, after stopping the traffic, I moved my helmet to the back of my head and took a series of photos. Suddenly I saw a lens moving into my face from the side and I heard the camera's shutter going. I looked to my side and saw a beaming smile on the face of a mate of mine who happened to be a press photographer for a national newspaper. He said, "I've gotcha." I threatened to seize his camera and had to make him promise not to put it in his paper, it cost me a pint of beer!

On another occasion Dave and I were walking up the street, with our hands behind our backs (a typical policeman stance) while the dancers were performing. We became aware that the entire audience were laughing at something behind us and when we looked around there was a procession of fools walking along behind us led by Stilton. We stopped and turned around and they all ran off.

One Sunday morning I was collecting all the cones in as usual when I slammed my thumb in the door of the van and crushed the top of it. After hospital treatment I returned to duty of sorts with my arm in a sling. Controlling the traffic at the church during the lunchtime dancing was interesting and my press photographer friend was about with his camera again. I had to ask him not to publish the shots, which cost me another pint of beer!

I have many other fond memories of Morris Weekend and these are just a few.

Criminal Damage With A Difference

Domestics were always the bane of my life whether they were between neighbours, husband and wife or family members, primarily because police powers are very limited. However one domestic I got involved in resulted in a prosecution.

It all began one morning when I came on duty at 09:00. The phone rang and a member of the public was reporting some graffiti on the path of an alley that ran from Copthall Lane to Magdalen Green and the primary school. I walked to the alley and was a little surprised with what I found. In bright yellow gloss paint, in large letters (about ½ a metre in size) painted on the tarmac surface and extending virtually the entire length of the alley were the words 'LILLIE HARRIS IS AN HORE' in block capitals. The person responsible had gone to a lot of effort, although their spelling and grammar left a little to be desired! I was unable to secure the services of a Scenes of Crime Officer to photograph the graffiti so I took a series of photographs on my camera.

Whilst there I was approached by a lady from nearby Bardfield Road, who informed me that there was writing on the road outside her house. I went with her and found the writing, this time in red gloss paint in even larger letters (almost a metre in size) this time saying 'L. HARRIS IS AN HOARE'. Again a lot of effort had gone into the writing and I was a little surprised that the paint had not run with all the traffic using this road. I could only surmise that it had been done in the middle of the night when there would have been no traffic. I took more photos before walking back to my office.

I then received a further call reporting some large lettering across the Sampford Road, out of the town. I attended and, sure enough, there it was again in red gloss paint. The lettering was even larger than the previous two patches. The words 'LILLIE HARRIS IS AN WHORE' extended right across the road - someone had been very busy last night. I took another series of photos, as I was still unable to locate a Scenes of Crime Officer, and met up with representatives from the local Highways Department. They were not happy, especially after I showed them all three patches. They arranged for a team to come out and remove the graffiti as a matter of urgency.

I knew Lillie Harris quite well, she was a lady in her early sixties, married with grown up children. What I didn't know was that she had been having an affair with a local man also in his sixties, a Bill Wyatt. The affair had been going on for over twenty years. Being the soul of discretion I called on Lillie while her husband was at work and had a chat with her over a cup of tea. She admitted the affair to me but stated that she had recently ended it, as Bill had taken to drink.

With the information from Lillie, who was very upset about the graffiti, I called on Bill who denied everything. I searched his garden shed where I found various tins of paint, which I took possession of. I then arrested Bill and took him to Saffron Walden Police Station, where he later admitted to all the graffiti. His explanation was that he had been upset at Lillie for breaking up the affair and he had gone out and got drunk. In the early hours had gone out with the paint. At the subsequent prosecution at the local Magistrates' Court I produced my photographs in evidence, which the magistrates appreciated. The chairman of the bench held up the folder of photographs in front of him and by the way the folder was shaking I am certain that he was chuckling to himself. Bill was fined £200 with a further £300 compensation to the local authority for the removal of all the graffiti. He was also 'bound over' for one year. Bill shook my hand as he left the court and said, "If I see you in the pub, I'll buy you a drink."

An Ace Detective

One evening I received a call from a resident of a remote cottage stating that he had come home to discover that the cottage had been broken into and a quantity of silver had been stolen. I attended the beautiful thatched cottage that I had not been inside before. I introduced myself and was shown into the sitting room, which was in a bit of a mess. The burglars had ransacked this room as well as throughout the cottage. As I looked around an ear-splitting whistle began and I became aware of a large green parrot sitting on a perch in the corner of the room. I spoke to the householder above the whistle, which continued incessantly and we were forced to move into another room to speak. The parrot's name was Ace and apparently he whistled/screeched like this every time a stranger came into the house.

I had requested a Scenes of Crime Officer (SOCO) to check for fingerprints and there was a trace of blood on the rear kitchen window, which had been smashed, and was the apparent point of entry by the burglars. With all the mess inside I assumed that there had been more than one burglar. I sat in the kitchen taking a statement and the parrot eventually stopped its ear shattering noise, only to start up again when the SOCO entered the room - needless to say he didn't stay in there for long. No fingerprints were found but the blood traces were taken though the science of DNA in criminal investigations was in its infancy.

Although details of the silver, including some very unusual hallmarks on some, and photographs were circulated nothing was heard until several months later. I received a phone call from Harlow CID informing me that they had two burglars in custody who were to admitting to jobs in my area.

Arrangements were made for the two to be brought over so I could go out with them and CID to see if they had committed any of my undetected dwelling burglaries. They were happy to admit any that were down to them, as they were keen to clear their sheet and to show the court that they had fully cooperated with the police. It was quite apparent that they had been busy in north west Essex and after travelling around for over half an hour we came up to the cottage that had lost the silver. As we approached one of the young men in the back said, "Yes that was us; there was a b....y parrot in there making a hell of a row." The two detectives looked at me in curiosity and I had to explain what they meant. This was the first burglary for which they had been detected partly by a parrot!

The two burglars eventually received lengthy custodial sentences at Chelmsford Crown Court. We did recover quite a lot of stolen property including some of the silver from Ace's home.

An Important Prisoner

Whilst working at Thaxted one was expected to help out at the local stations from time to time, for me that meant the Saffron Walden and Dunmow Police Stations.

One year the Chief Inspector at Saffron Walden decided to have an Open Day when the public would be invited in to look around the station and look at a number of displays that he wanted put on. This would serve as a Public Relations exercise, to show the public what goes on behind the scenes.

Several meetings were held to sort out the day and the various displays and activities. Initially I was not given a specific task but as the plans came together I was given the cell block to show people around. If they requested it I was to shut them in a cell for a brief moment to give them an idea of what it was like to be 'locked up'.

After a lot of planning the day eventually arrived. There were some excellent displays inside and outside the building, including a huge glass-fronted tank in the front yard, full of water, which the force diving team used to demonstrate their work. Traffic Department had brought over a very smart car, and there was a lot more going on.

Many people attended and, I believe, thoroughly enjoyed themselves, especially the kids who were particularly interested in the cells. When the big steel door slammed shut with them inside, it quietened them down and their facial expressions said it all. Many parents would have been happy for them to remain in there!

During the early afternoon a surprise visitor arrived - the Chief Constable and his wife had decided to visit the station. The rather surprised Chief Inspector showed them around and they appeared to be very impressed. Eventually they arrived at the cell complex and spoke to me. The Chief's wife was interested in seeing the inside of the cell and as we walked out she was sitting on the bench. The Chief turned to me with a cheeky smile and said, "Shut the door". I slammed the door shut and looked through the hatch, as the chief walked away and disappeared. She simply sat there looking around the four bare walls. I opened the door and she came out and said, "I suppose my husband told you to shut me in." I smiled and said nothing. As she walked away she smiled and said, "One wouldn't want to be in there for too long, thank you very much for letting me out."

Found Property With A Difference

One August bank holiday I was on duty with Dave Kinnley. We had covered the usual bank holiday Morris Dancing at Thaxted Church and returned to my office for a cup of tea when the phone rang. My control at HQ had received a report that a balloon had come down on a farm at Little Sampford. They asked if we could attend and assess the situation. We set off for the farm with Cassie in the back - she often came out with me. I assumed that the balloon was either a weather balloon or a hot air balloon. I was therefore a little surprised when we arrived at the farm and spoke to the farmer. He advised us that the balloon had 'bounced' from one field to another where he and his men had managed to catch it in the strong wind that was blowing.

We walked with the farmer to a field behind some barns where I was astonished to find a large red and white barrage balloon with the words 'PINE SELL DIRECT' in bold lettering down each side. The balloon was floating in the air above a tractor to which it was tied with a steel cable that ran from the balloon. Cassie was very nervous and stayed close to my feet.

A second nylon cable ran from the balloon and was wrapped around the steel one. We assumed that this cable was attached to a release valve on the underside of the balloon but, try as we might, it would not open the valve. I contacted control and asked them what we should do with it. I received the classic reply, "What do you normally do with found property? Take it back to your office and enter it in your Found Property Register." Dave and I looked at each other and scratched our heads. The balloon was about four metres long with large inflated tail fins!

We eventually decided to tie it securely to the roof of the police car. To do this we had to fold all the aerials down on the roof. Using the steel hawser on the balloon and a rope from the farmer we secured it to the roof. We then drove very slowly back to the office, the tail of the balloon hanging down the back of the car, though I had clear vision at the front. As we drove up through the High Street, our 'load' turned a few heads. As we arrived at the office the phone was ringing and I answered it. The male voice at the other end said, "Is that the police? I want to report that I lost my balloon." I suspected that someone was playing a prank and my suspicions were realised when the guy burst out laughing, it was a friend of mine who lived in the High Street.

We removed the balloon but still couldn't get it down so we pushed it into the garage and shut the door. I then made enquiries to trace the company and it was later established that the balloon had broken away from its moorings over a factory in Gamlingay in Bedfordshire. It was later signed for and collected and I do believe that the company got into trouble with the Civil Aviation Authority for contravening controlled air space!

In At The Deep End

As the years went on I began to perform more and more duties as acting Sergeant, including a long stretch at Saffron Walden. On my very first duty there I was on early turn; at about 07:00 we received a call from Great Chesterford Railway Station informing us that they had a possible chemical incident with a leaking tanker on the tracks. The tanker had been moved into a siding which was close to a main road.

We attended, but didn't get too close, and I arranged for the road to be closed. Officers from the British Transport Police were en route to deal with the tanker along with the Fire Brigade who, on their arrival, immediately set up a full chemical incident. We were engaged with the road closure and keeping the media at a safe distance for most of the morning. The road closure had caused chaos for the commuters with a long detour. The end result was that the chemical was a fairly innocuous one, but no chances could be taken.

The very next day a call was taken by one of the shift as we drank a cup of tea first thing. I was asked to ring a Mr. L. E. Fant after 10:00 and was given the number. When I rang it was Whipsnade Zoo! I had been well and truly 'had' - the joys of leadership. From then on I was on my guard.

Towards the end of this week of early turns I was to experience the over-enthusiasm of one of the younger members of the shift - a probationer who had four months in service and was very keen. I had put him out on foot patrol in the town centre, with a special officer. It was the school's half term and the town was busy.

Halfway through the morning the radio burst into action. The probationer had arrested four boys and was bringing them in. I offered him a car to assist but he declined. A few minutes later there was a bang at the back door. There stood my probationer with the boys. He frogmarched them into the custody area; I looked at the special who looked at me and shrugged his shoulders.

As is customary when a person is arrested, the arresting officer must explain to them directly why they have been arrested. These four had been detained for gambling in a public place - they were playing cards in a bus stop as it was raining and they had given the PC some lip when he had spoken to them. When I asked them how old they were they all stated that they were nine years old, which placed them under the age of criminal responsibility. Why had I volunteered for this 'acting Sergeant' lark? I took the PC to one side and advised him that they were under age - he hadn't thought to ask them how old they were!

I immediately put all four boys in the back of a police car and took them to their respective homes; two of the lads were twins. I spoke to the parents who were all very understanding and appreciated our concern for their sons' welfare. The matter was closed. I did not inform the Duty Inspector as this would have got the young PC into trouble, I did however take the PC out for a 'chat'!

That week of earlies proved to be a nightmare for me, but if nothing else came out of it, the young probationer learnt a salutary lesson in common sense.

An Old Fashioned Pub Brawl

Pub fights were always a village bobby's worst nightmare, because generally he or she was the first on the scene and it always seemed like an age before back up arrived. This scenario happened to me one Sunday afternoon when I was on duty.

The day had been quiet and I had managed to get some outstanding enquiries completed; Sundays were always good days for enquiries as people were invariably at home. I had just finished a shotgun certificate application when a call went up, "Any unit for a major disturbance at the Fox and Hounds public house at Thaxted". I acknowledged and told control that I would attend - I was about five minutes away – and other units were sent to back me up.

On my arrival the scene that greeted me in the bar was one of total devastation. There were bodies lying everywhere - one was lying across the bar with his head partially in the sink, another lay behind the bar in amongst the shattered remains of a bar mirror and the optics. Chairs were smashed, tables tipped over. In amongst all this were two men sitting at the bar finishing a drink. I knew these two men as a father and son from Thaxted, who were very handy with their fists.

There were a total of nine unconscious or semi-conscious men at various locations around the bar. A very nervous licensee came up to me and told me that the two men were having a quiet drink at the bar, when this gang of men, who he believed were squaddies from the local barracks, had picked on the two. One had no hair, as he had alopecia (a hair loss complaint) and they thought he was a skinhead. A fight broke out and all nine of the squaddies were laid out. He described it as being like a fight in a cowboy western film but without the guns.

I tendered what first aid I could until a fleet of ambulances and police cars arrived. I then spoke to the two at the bar who, apart from red knuckles, did not have a scratch on them. They confirmed what the licensee had said, that the squaddies had started the fight and these two had simply defended themselves, by the looks of it, very well!

The officers and ambulance crews that backed me up were amazed at the devastation but, miraculously, there were no serious injuries except for a couple of broken noses and a broken jaw. I took the two men into Saffron Walden to obtain statements from them to try and draw a picture as to exactly what had happened; the licensee also came in to make a statement. The barracks were informed that nine of their men had been taken off to hospital.

On subsequent interview of the nine army personnel, their stories more or less bore out what the other witnesses had said - the bottom line being that it had been their fault. They had been drinking for most of the day at various pubs, as it was one of their group's birthday and they hadn't been in this pub long.

A few days later an army lorry pulled up outside my office and the nine were frogmarched into my office. They all had black eyes and bruised faces. They were made to apologise to me individually and I did feel a little sorry for them. They were then marched back onto the lorry though the Guard Commander stayed behind. He asked me what was going to happen to these nine in respect of any proceedings and whether they could make restitution to the licensee. I advised him that as far as a prosecution of them went a decision would have to be made by the Crown Prosecution Service, but if full restitution were made to the licensee, that might help.

Full restitution to the licensee was made and the nine helped to clear up and repaint the bar. I hate to think what the cost was to them. In view of this, and the fact that they were to be disciplined by the military, the Crown Prosecution Service decided that it would not be in the public interest to prosecute the soldiers. I was more than happy with the result, as I did not want them court marshalled and thrown out of the army. My Chief Inspector received a letter from the men's Commanding Officer thanking us for the way that we dealt with this incident; my boss was very pleased.

Drink Driving

One beautiful sunny afternoon Cassie and I were out in the police car. We had popped into Saffron Walden to drop off some paperwork and were on our way back to my office when we came up behind a car travelling in the same direction. The car was weaving all over the road.

As we reached a fairly sharp right-hand bend, known locally as Gunters Corner, I saw the driver take a drink from a can. As he did so the car swerved violently across the central white line. As I watched I saw him take another long drink from the can and again the car swerved erratically – fortunately there was no approaching traffic.

I put the blue lights on and when the driver saw me in his rear view mirror he looked very surprised. I could see him put the can under his seat and the car swerved again before he pulled over and came to a stop. I got out and left Cassie guarding the car. The driver was just sitting looking straight ahead as I walked up to his car. I indicated for him to open the window but he just sat there. I banged hard on the glass and eventually the window opened and the driver looked at me and slurred, "Is there a problem officer?"

I noticed a number of empty beer cans in the passenger foot well and said, "By your manner of driving I believe you have been consuming alcohol." This was all rather academic really as I had seen him drinking. He replied, "I have had one officer, I was thirsty." I asked him to step out of the car, which he did with some difficulty. He was having a problem even standing up and had to lean against the car.

Now, in those days the breathalyser was the crystal tube with a mouthpiece at one end and a bag at the other that had to be inflated. We had to wait 20 minutes after his last drink before providing the breath sample. I eventually gave him the breathalyser and told him that I wanted him to fully inflate the bag in one breath. It was with some difficulty that he blew into the tube but eventually the bag was expanded. The crystals in the tube were yellow and if there was alcohol they would turn a pale green. In this sample the crystals turned a very dark green!

I arrested him and placed him in the back of the police car. Cassie knew the routine and moved to the front passenger seat. I was then joined by another double-crewed car and they brought the man's car in.

The subsequent tests revealed that the man was five times over the legal limit. He was eventually fined £500 and banned from driving for five years. This was his second conviction – some people never learn.

The Warning That Was Ignored

Another incident involving army personnel occurred soon after the fight, but it didn't involve the same men - fortunately.

One evening a Churchwarden from Thaxted Church called at my office. He was complaining about three soldiers that were courting three local Thaxted girls. They were using the south porch of the Church and making a lot of mess with cigarette ends and discarded food wrappings.

He had asked them to find somewhere else to do their courting, but they had ignored his request.

The following evening I was on duty and decided to put on my helmet and go for a walk with Cassie. We wandered down to the Church and around to the south porch. Shining my torch in I startled three men and three girls, all in various states of undress. The men initially did not realise who was behind the torch and became very abusive. I then shone my torch onto my face and helmet and all went very quiet! They apologised, quickly sorted out their clothes, got up and left. I warned them not to come back and that if they did I would contact the barracks.

The following night was a repetition, but this time I left them in no uncertain terms that if they came back again there would be trouble; they told me that they wouldn't return.

A few nights later I was off duty and was out giving Cassie a late night walk. We walked down to the Church and, as I walked across the car park at the western end of the Church, I heard voices coming from the south porch. I gave it a wide berth but it was obvious that the group that I had asked to leave before were back. I could hear male and female voices and lots of giggling. I could see the bright glowing ends of cigarettes - I was not very happy!

The following day, I met the Churchwarden at the south porch. There was a large amount of litter: cigarette ends, fish and chip papers and empty beer cans strewn around. The Churchwarden had cleared a lot of mess from the porch every morning.

That night I came on duty at 21:30 specifically to deal with this problem once and for all. I wandered down to the Church and I could hear the familiar noise coming from the porch. I contacted Saffron Walden Police and apprised them of the situation. I asked them to contact the duty guard at the barracks and a short while later a large army truck arrived. A number of soldiers jumped out and I told the senior officer the situation. I advised him that I had spoken to them before but they had chosen to ignore my warnings.

They all disappeared around the back of the Church. There was some shouting from the senior officer and soon afterwards the three men were being frog-marched back to the truck where they were unceremoniously placed. The three girls walked off crying.

The following morning sharp at 09:00 I heard a loud bang at the office door. I went through and there, standing at the door, was a very senior officer from the barracks, who I knew. He came in and apologised for the behaviour of his men. He then went out and the three soldiers were marched into the office with an escort and told to apologise to me, which they did. They were then marched out. I told the senior officer that I would inform the Church authorities and asked him what was going to happen to the soldiers. He advised me that they were appearing in front of the Commanding Officer tomorrow and I told him that the matter was closed as far as I was concerned.

Again, I felt a little sorry for them really, but I had warned them. I later learnt that the Commanding Officer had forced the men to apologise to the vicar and to spend a week clearing up the Churchyard and tidying up the graves - the Churchyard had never looked so pristine. Some good came out of this incident.

Robbery

Mid-morning one day I was on duty in my office completing some paperwork when a call went up for a unit to attend an attempted robbery at a shop in Thaxted that had just occurred. I responded immediately and drove quickly down to the shop. I met the lady who was very upset. She told me that a man had come into the shop wearing a balaclava and brandishing a knife. He had demanded money and held a knife at the lady's two children, threatening to kill them if she didn't pay up. She said to him, "Don't be stupid Alan", as she recognised the man to be Alan Wilson, David Wilson's brother. I was curious as to how she had recognised him and she stated that he had cut the eye holes so big that she knew it was him; he was a regular customer in the shop!

I left the shop and started to search for Alan. Halfway up Orange Street I found the balaclava lying on the footpath. I drove around to the estate where Alan lived and, sure enough, there he was running back to his house. I accelerated and pulled up ahead of him. He stopped and put his hands on his head. I arrested him, searched him and found a large Sabatier kitchen knife up his sleeve.

On interview he admitted the robbery, but was curious as to how the lady had recognised him. I informed him that he had cut the eye holes too big and the shop owner had recognised him. He smiled and said something that I will not repeat.

At his subsequent trial he was sent to prison for three years. He was incarcerated at a local prison in Suffolk and soon after his arrival he asked to see me. I arranged a police prison visit with a local CID Officer and was curious as to why Alan wanted to see me, but it soon became clear. He wanted to clear his 'sheet' and admitted his involvement in a number of thefts and burglaries also implicating his two brothers and some other youths in Thaxted - he even told me where a lot of the stolen property was hidden. We cleared up quite a few outstanding crimes in the area and recovered a lot of stolen property – our detection figures were looking pretty good!

An Early Morning Walk

One morning I was on an early turn at Great Dunmow helping them out because they were short of manpower. At the briefing we learnt that the night shift had been sent to an alarm at a garage on the outskirts of the town in the early hours. On their arrival they saw a car speeding away and gave chase. They saw the car in the distance as it sped off towards Chelmsford, around a series of bends known locally as the Barnston bends. After a high speed chase over several miles the car was eventually stopped and a few packets of cigarettes were found in the vehicle; the three male occupants were arrested.

The garage owner had been contacted and had attended. He reported a large quantity of cigarettes missing along with some cans of drink and the video from the surveillance cameras. The point of entry had been via a smashed window immediately in front of one of the cameras.

The arresting officers felt that the men in custody may have thrown the stolen property, including the film, out of the car when it was out of sight of the pursuing police car. The early turn Sergeant had been requested to arrange for the hedgerow and ditch from the garage to where the car was stopped to be searched thoroughly. The only way that this could be carried out was on foot and yes, you have guessed it, I got the job. There was only the Sergeant, a probationer and myself on that morning.

So off I set with a high visibility jacket and my helmet on. It was a lovely spring morning with a strong westerly breeze and small clouds scudding across the sky. Traffic was heavy as the rush hour gathered pace - once or twice I even had to leap into the bushes! I walked and walked along the verge but couldn't find anything. I continued on through Hounslow Green and on towards Ford End, eventually reaching the spot where we had been informed the car had been stopped. I had been walking for two hours with no result.

I walked across the road and began walking back towards Dunmow. The traffic had eased but the breeze had increased. As before I was leaping in and out of the hedge and the ditch but as the search continued I was becoming more and disheartened; I began to think that this was all a waste of time.

On and on I walked, amazed at just how much rubbish collected in a roadside ditch next to a busy road. I was just entering the bends again when I suddenly spotted a cigarette packet in the ditch in a stretch where there was no hedge. On further investigation I discovered that it was unopened. With gloves on, to preserve any fingerprint evidence, I carefully picked the packet up and placed it in a plastic evidence bag. Was this one of the stolen packets?

I walked a little further on with raised spirits and there, lying in the ditch, were numerous packets of cigarettes including a packet of 200 still in their cellophane. I had struck gold and was feeling quite pleased with myself. I bagged up the find and called up Dunmow control to inform them what I had found. I was told to see if the video film was nearby.

About a quarter of a mile from where I had found the cigarettes I found the video deep under the hedge - that made my day. I bagged it up, called it in and was told to check the remaining stretch back to the garage, which I did. The Sergeant was waiting for me at the garage in a police car; he was delighted with my find. All the evidence was entered up when I got back and sent off for forensic examination.

About nine months later I received a court warning to attend Chelmsford Crown Court, for the trial of the men involved in the burglary. They were pleading not guilty and I couldn't really see how they were entering this plea, but I was soon to discover why. On the second day of the trial I was in the box and I got quite a grilling. The defence barristers were accusing me of planting the evidence, which was absolutely ridiculous. I asked the barristers how they thought I got hold of the stolen video to plant it. The barristers continued their onslaught for almost an hour, attempting to discredit my evidence and trying to create an element of doubt in the minds of the jury; eventually the judge intervened and supported me.

At the end of the trial the men were found guilty on all charges. It then transpired that all the men had previous convictions for burglaries on petrol filling stations, in fact they had committed some garage burglaries while they were on bail for the Dunmow offence. They were sent to prison for long terms. After the men left and the jury were dismissed, the judge turned to me in the witness gallery and commented on my perseverance in the search, I was quite chuffed!

'Head First'

It was very late one evening, I was off duty watching the TV with Cassie, my Jack Russell terrier on my lap when the phone rang. A local resident was reporting a road accident in Park Street, Thaxted, she did not know if anyone was injured. I grabbed my coat and went to get the Police car keys, Cassie was already waiting at the office door, she knew I was going out and she was not going to miss the excitement. She leapt into the Police car and sat in her usual place, up on the back shelf.

We were on scene at accident shortly after. I was quite amazed with what I found. A small high performance saloon car had gone head first into a shop window and was embedded in the shop. The driver and passenger were still in the car. There were a number of people looking on but no one thought about trying to get them out. There was a strong smell of petrol coming from the car so I requested fire brigade. I climbed into the shop and quickly helped the badly shaken driver out of the vehicle and then got the passenger out, it was mother and daughter; they were shaken but not injured. I got them well away from the shop and the onlookers. My traffic colleagues soon arrived and sorted out the accident and the recovery of the vehicle once the brigade made it safe, it was a tricky business removing the vehicle. Cassie remained in the vehicle and watched intently.

The young driver was a learner and it transpired that she had turned into Park Street and had hit the accelerator instead of the brake, lost control and 'entered' the shop.

The name of the shop was appropriately 'Head First'!

'Charlie's Away'

If there is one rural activity that arouses strong emotions it is fox hunting. At the time of writing this section hunting with hounds has been banned by statute for two years. The stories I am about to relate to occurred over the 28 years that I policed the five different hunts that hunted in Essex.

During the hunting season the hunts would meet some weekdays and on Saturdays. We very rarely had problems on the weekday meets but the Saturday meets would attract the attention of people of all ages who would protest against the hunt, sometimes peacefully, but more often by actively trying to disrupt the hunt. We named these protestors 'sabs' - short for saboteurs - or 'antis'. Our role was to allow both activities to take place as peaceful protest and hunting were both lawful activities. This was a regular activity for the police on Saturdays during the winter months, from October to March. I have many memories of hunting and the following are just a brief glimpse at just a few. Before I start I should acquaint the reader with a few hunting terms:

The Hunt Master is the huntsman in overall charge of the hunt. Hounds are the dogs used in fox hunting. The Whipper In is the huntsman in charge of the hounds. The Field is the term used for the group of horses and riders with the hunt that day. The Terrier Man is the man employed by the hunt to work the terriers to flush foxes if they go to ground or up pipes or tunnels. The Followers are the members of the public that watch and follow the hunt.

"Charlie's Away" is the term that is often shouted when a fox breaks cover. An Earth is the home of a fox. The Meet is where the hunt gathers before they commence hunting. Gone to Earth is the term used when a fox disappears in to a hole, or earth, in the ground.

One hunt meet that I will never forget, and possibly one of the most problematical, occurred quite a few years ago now and involved a meet on the Essex/Hertfordshire border at Rickling Green. The meet was in a farmyard and comprised over thirty horses. I was acting Sergeant and was in company with PC Trevor Bailey, an experienced hunting officer and a good friend of many years. We also had three officers from Harlow; hunting was a new activity for them but they were to learn a lot that day.

We checked around the immediate area to see if there were any sabs' vehicles parked up, but there were none. Were we going to have a quiet day?

The hunt moved off across the fields behind the farm and towards a lane and wood beyond. Suddenly from out of nowhere three vans full of sabs arrived. They parked up and decamped; they looked quite a sight as they appeared, all dressed in black and wearing black balaclavas. The idea of this clothing was to cause problems in identification of individuals if offences occurred. The sabs immediately ran across the field, squirting aniseed onto the ground to confuse the hounds and blowing a hunting horn. I should point out that at this time civil trespass was not a police matter, this was set to change in the early 1990s. I sent two officers with Trevor to monitor the situation.

The hounds soon cleared the wood with no foxes found and the Whipper In blew his horn and gathered the hounds in. He then led the hounds across the field and the horses followed. The sabs ran back to their vans - I counted thirty as our control wanted to know how many we had - back up was on its way from headquarters. Trevor and I then spoke to all the sabs and warned them that if they continued their behaviour they were likely to be arrested.

The hunt had ridden off and the hounds were drawing some rough cover. The sabs left in a hurry and we followed. They were equipped with maps and CB radios and were soon ahead of the hunt. They all decamped from the vans and ran across the fields towards the hunt. A man came up to us who we knew - he was on the hunt committee. He demanded that we stop these 'hooligans' and we told him that we had no authority. He stomped off across the field and walked through the line of sabs who had stopped in the middle of the field. We heard him shout some comment to them which they ignored. He had only gone a little way ahead of the sabs when they began running towards the hounds that had appeared from the cover. The man turned and put his arms in the air indicating for them to stop, but they didn't. The next thing we saw was the man laying flat on the ground with his arms sticking straight up into the air and the sabs running towards the hounds beyond him.

The man got up, looked at us and then ran after the sabs. The Whipper In had obviously seen the approaching crowd and had decided to beat a hasty retreat with the pack. I sent Trevor and some others down to the sabs who had turned around and were approaching a group of huntsmen nearby. The next thing I saw was one of the huntsmen being dragged from his horse by two of the sabs, who were immediately arrested by two of the Harlow officers. They were handcuffed and brought back to the police cars and placed in the back. The remaining sabs came running back to their vans parked nearby. I informed police control of the arrests and requested urgent backup, along with the fact that we were now near the village of Meesden in the Hertfordshire Police district! The sabs returned to their vehicles giving the thumbs up to their two colleagues with us.

They drove off and we followed. On the outskirts of Meesden we stopped as the hounds were in a wood near the road. The sabs leapt out and ran towards the wood spraying the aniseed and blowing the hunting horn in an attempt to draw the hounds away again. Suddenly one of the followers on the road in front of us shouted, "Charlie's Away, Charlie's away" and waved his cap in the air. From our vantage point we could see the fox running across the field before disappearing behind some houses. The hounds had picked up the scent and were in full cry after the animal. At this point a double crewed Hertfordshire car arrived. I apprised them of the situation and requested that they took the two arrested sabs into a police station for processing. They agreed, solving one problem.

Just after the Hertfordshire unit left a very distressed, middle-aged lady came running up to us shouting, "They have killed my mother, they have killed my mother. You must come please." At that point I heard two-tone sirens approaching and assumed that it was another police car arriving, but an ambulance appeared at the end of the road and stopped outside a nearby house. Trevor and I went over to the house with the lady. We went in and on the sitting room floor was an elderly lady lying prone, with the ambulance crew working on her. She appeared to regain consciousness and began crying uncontrollably. The ambulance crew managed to calm her down and she then told us, amidst the tears, that the hunt had killed her cat on the back lawn. Trevor and I, with the old lady's daughter, went out onto the back lawn where we could see a large patch of blood and fur in the middle of the lawn. However when we examined it closely it was apparent to us that the fur was that of a fox, not a cat. When we returned to the house and walked through the kitchen door a ginger cat suddenly ran into the kitchen through our legs.

By then the old lady was sitting on a chair so we spoke to her and informed her that her cat was safe. She had been standing in the sitting room when she suddenly saw the hounds appear through the hedge and run across the lawn to kill what she thought was her cat. She didn't remember anything else until the ambulance crew revived her. As she had a serious heart condition the ambulance crew took her out to the ambulance and into hospital for a check up. As Trevor and I were leaving the house, a Hertfordshire unit arrived with the Duty Inspector. I apprised him of the situation and he requested more manpower but, with a major demonstration in Hertford, he was desperately short of resources. He asked us if we could remain with the hunt for the time being and as we stood there talking the three sabs' vehicles went roaring past us.

We were then contacted by our control stating that Hertfordshire control had received a number of 999 calls reporting a major disturbance at the hunt. We attended and the scene that greeted us was one of total chaos. Several of the huntsmen were off their horses and fighting with the sabs, whose numbers had swollen with the arrival of a few more vehicles full of protesters. Many were in combat clothing and as they were not wearing balaclavas Trevor and I recognised many of them from previous hunts. Almost immediately two Essex Police personnel carriers arrived and the fight was broken up. I ended up requesting an ambulance for two of the sabs that were injured - I could see blood oozing out from under their balaclavas. When I took the balaclavas off I discovered that both were females and had some nasty facial injuries. Several arrests were made including two huntsmen - the Inspector had arrested one of them! The main offences that they were arrested for were breaching the peace and assault.

The hunt was abandoned for the day so I suppose that the sabs had achieved what they wanted. Trevor and I ended up at Hertford Police Station making statements. It was ironic really that more arrests had been made at the hunt than at the demonstration in Hertford town.

The old lady who collapsed made a full recovery and received a visit from the Hunt Master with a bouquet of flowers and an apology. Most of the people arrested were convicted for a range of offences. The Essex Chief Constable received a long letter of thanks from the Hertfordshire Chief Constable. These events were typical of a hunting day.

Another incident involved the Essex Fire and Rescue Service. After a long, wet November the hunt were out one Saturday near Christmas. It was very wet and the field was small; unusually we had no sabs. Dave Kinnley and I were out together and remained with the hunt all day, as sabs could turn up at any time.

Towards the end of the day the hounds were drawing a copse near a field of sugar beet, which was between the copse and the road where we were parked. The hounds suddenly found the strong scent of a fox and were running in full cry. For the horses to follow they needed to jump a deep ditch that had recently been cleaned out. As we watched we suddenly saw a beautiful 18 hands high grey hunter slip on the top of the ditch and slide into the ditch, throwing the rider onto the bank. It was soon apparent that the horse had not come out of the ditch. A number of the riders had dismounted and were either in the ditch or standing on top looking down. There was obviously a serious problem, so Dave and I went to investigate.

I got a shock when we looked down into the ditch, as the sight was dramatic and incredible. The horse was upside down in the ditch with its four legs sticking up into the air - it was well and truly stuck. The more it struggled the more it seemed to get set in the V of the ditch. Everyone knew that time was of the essence if the horse was to survive. I suggested to the gathering that a vet and the fire brigade be called and it was agreed. I went back to the police car and informed my control of the situation. Within a short space of time the local fire brigade were on the scene and the crew were trudging across the mud with a small generator and lighting as the daylight was rapidly fading. A local vet also attended and was very pessimistic that the horse would survive. The fire crew had requested the attendance of a heavy lifting appliance from Chelmsford. There was little more we could do until the lifting gear arrived, which it did in record time.

I was a little concerned as to how the huge, heavy tender was going to get to the horse, but I need not have worried for it literally drove across the field leaving deep trenches in its wake. Trenches were dug out of the banks on either side of the horse to enable wide webbing straps to be passed underneath the animal. Eventually all the straps were in place, the lifting arm was swung over and the straps were attached. To prevent the horse from struggling and turning prematurely we all took hold of a leg as it slowly began to lift. Up and up it came, and when it was clear of the ditch it was lowered down onto the ground. The horse slowly got to its feet, albeit a little unsteady and covered in mud. The vet checked him over before he was led away and everybody was very relieved.

Now the problem was how to get the tender back to the road, as the pressure of lifting the horse had caused it to sink even further into the field. The farmer and owner of the sugar beet field offered to bring a tractor to pull it out -

I suggested that it might need more than one. In the event it took four large tractors pulling together to get it back to the road. It brought half the field with it and deposited it on the road. Highways had to be requested to clear the road after everybody left! Dave and I got home at 21:30 several hours after we were due off. The horse did make a full recovery which was more than could be said for the sugar beet field.

A Speeding Ticket To Regret

For many years the main road running through Thaxted was the A130, but after the opening of the M11 from Junction 8 to Junction 10 the A130 was downgraded to the B184. The upside of this was that we lost a lot of the lorries coming through Thaxted, but the spin off was that we had an increase in the incidents of speeding cars into and through the town. The speed limit was 30 mph past my office at the northern end of the town and through the town.

Complaints began pouring in, from residents within the speed restricted area, to myself and my senior officers. The Traffic Division attended on a number of occasions and caught quite a few motorists but the complaints continued. My Inspector at Saffron Walden Police Station decided that to support the traffic department in their efforts in Thaxted, myself and a number of local officers would stage a series of speed checks outside my office.

These proved to be very successful and were staged at various times during the day. The busiest times were 07:00

to 09:00 and 17:00 to 19:00. These checks had the desired effect of slowing motorists down, so we achieved our goal, and a couple of checks were memorable.

One evening I was carrying out some checks on my own outside my office. I saw the lights of a car approaching and registered its speed as 43 mph. The vehicle passed me and I pulled out behind it. After a quick flash of blue lights the vehicle pulled over and a young lady emerged as I got out of the police car. I intended to give her a warning about her speed and she was very apologetic.

I issued her with a ticket to produce her driving documents within seven days and was in the process of warning her about her speed, when suddenly my loose-fitting denture plate flew out and shattered on the path where we were standing; teeth from the plate went flying everywhere. There was a stunned silence and then both of us burst into laughter. She took her ticket, got back into her car, still laughing, and drove off, leaving me to collect up my teeth!

On the very last day of these checks, I decided that we would do two checks, one early in the morning and one in the early evening. We started at 07:00 with four of us plus the Inspector manning the check, using a radar gun supplied by the Traffic Division. We had stopped a number of cars when I suddenly spotted a small saloon car approaching and accelerating into the speed limit; I registered its speed at 45 mph and signalled for the car to stop. It pulled over into the lay by and it was at this point that I recognised the driver as a nursing friend of mine, Pat. We were on a number of local committees together in Thaxted and she was the local Girl Guide leader. While the Inspector checked her car over I spoke to her and issued a Fixed Penalty Ticket for the speeding offence. This meant that she would have to pay a fine of £40 and three points would be placed on her driving licence; she did not look very happy when she drove off. In the evening I caught my dentist, a local television celebrity and a couple of local dignitaries - a good day all around!

Giving Pat those three points was destined to come back and haunt me. Within twelve months Pat and I were living together. I had bought a Land Rover and she wanted to go on my insurance as a named driver. The insurance company agreed and needed a copy of her licence, which I duly sent to them. When they saw the three points on her licence, which in effect I had given her, they loaded me up £100 on my premium. When I told them how she got the three points, they thought the story was most amusing - I didn't! I still had to pay the excess and Pat had got her own back on me!

Pat is now my wife and we still talk about this incident. She says, "It serves you right" - I will leave you to draw your own conclusions

Schools Liaison Officer

Soon after moving to Thaxted, I introduced myself to the two local primary schools on my beat, namely Thaxted and Great Sampford. In those days the force placed a lot of emphasis on local police officers working in schools. We had three presentations we were supposed to give each term – Never Go With Strangers, The Green Cross Code and The Police, which was the story of policy throughout history to modern day policing. We used to show a film entitled The Challenge of a Lifetime.

The Stranger talk was always a difficult one as it was an important message that we needed to get across but without terrifying the kids. Every time I gave this talk my phone would ring in the evening from anxious parents asking why I had given the talk and if there was a problem they should know about – I often felt that they needed the talk as well!

As the years went by I found myself more and more involved with these two schools as well as with the neighbouring schools in Debden and Radwinter. I began to run courses for Cycling Proficiency at all four schools and became an examiner as well.

I had a number of amusing/memorable incidents while teaching the kids to ride their bikes properly. The kids had to be nine or ten years old before they could undertake a course. Prior to them starting parental consent had to be given and the bikes examined. We were checking for compulsory items - front and rear brakes (you would be surprised at how many came in with no brakes at all!), a bell and rear reflector. The faults that I found ranged from no brakes to bald tyres, loose handlebars and saddles to the wrong size bike for the individual (this was a fairly common occurrence as parents would buy bikes for their child to 'grow into'). Some youngsters could not touch the ground without leaning the bike over and this was very dangerous. As I pointed out to quite a few parents, their child may not live to grow into their bike – a shock tactic that usually worked.

Local cycle repair shops used to love it when I ran these courses. In Great Sampford there was a little old man who ran a cycle repair workshop in his back garden, almost opposite the school. I am sure that the local parents thought I was on commission!

The courses themselves were basically divided into two parts: the first part was in the playground, cycling through cones slowly to demonstrate that they could control the bike at slow speeds. They also had to learn the Highway Code part on cycling along with all the road signs. Then it was out on the road, learning procedures such as starting, stopping, turning right and left, slowing down and of course the dreaded emergency stop.

I remember one lad performing an emergency stop but he forgot to pull both brakes and applied the front brake only. He was catapulted through the air but fortunately was uninjured as he was wearing his helmet.

Another incident involved a young girl at Debden School. We were coming to the end of the course and their exam was looming (I did not examine my own students for obvious reasons). I had sent off a small group to cycle down the hill from the school to the Fox crossroads, where they were to dismount, turn around and come back. Eventually three out of four returned. When I enquired where the girl was no-one knew. She had ridden on ahead of the group.

I left a colleague who was learning the ropes with the main group and drove off in search of the girl. I don't mind admitting that I was really panicking. I reached the Fox crossroads and went on towards Saffron Walden. About a quarter of a mile further on I saw the familiar high visibility jacket riding merrily on towards the town – what a relief that was. It turned out that she had misunderstood my instructions. I let her ride back to school and followed in the car. Needless to say, she and all the other passed the test with flying colours.

I was treated like a member of staff at Thaxted School which became a regular tea stop. The Headteacher asked me on one occasion whether I would be interested in accompanying him and some other members of staff on a residential trip to the Isle of Wight. The kids were ten years old, in their final year at primary school and they all knew me well. I was going primarily as a naturalist as well as an extra member of staff.

We were staying in a hotel in Sandown but what the kids didn't know was that each room had an intercom with the main control in the bar. Every evening, unbeknownst to the children, we would listen to them. We heard some interesting jokes and found out what they thought of us. We also heard the 'midnight feasts' taking place.

I had my own room and one night I had a little note pushed under my door. It was addressed to James. I opened it and discovered that it was a love note, to James from the daughter of a colleague of mine. The following morning I took her to one side and gave her the note back. She blushed and said, "Please don't tell my mum and dad, please." I promised her that I would not and I never have.

Another incident on this trip involved the pier. We were given a group of ten mixed youngsters for the week and basically they were our responsibility. The Headteacher had briefed us on the first night that he felt it appropriate that our groups did not go onto the pier as there was a danger that they might spend too much of their £10 allowance, which was the maximum they were allowed to bring.

On our last full day there were a number of memorable incidents that occurred. My group wanted to go down to the shops to buy some presents for their parents. We went down as a group and visited a number of the seafront gift shops. At one shop a lad asked if he could pop in as he had seen something in the window. I told him that we would stay outside and wait for him but after five minutes there was no sign of him. I popped into the shop to chase him up and began to panic when I couldn't find him. I realised there was a back entrance and raced out of the door. There was the lad waiting patiently – what a relief!

We had agreed that as this was the last day and we were going to be in the coach for a long time tomorrow, we would go on a walk up on the cliffs above the town. Unfortunately I got my sense of direction wrong and we ended up walking off in the opposite direction to the main group. After a while I felt that something was wrong, so with my binoculars I scanned to the top of the cliffs and spotted the others way off in the distance. We eventually rejoined the main group and as we walked I explained about the fulmars that were gliding along the cliff edge and the variety of butterflies that we saw – it was a lovely walk.

That evening after supper the Headteacher said that if we wanted to take our groups out for an evening walk he had no objections; of course my group were up for it. We walked along the seafront to the pier where I received some serious nagging to go onto the pier. As it was their last night I could see no harm in it so I agreed. I limited the time to ten minutes but the slot machines gobbled up their money and I ended up lending them all extra cash. I had a go on the pinball, which I really enjoy, and my group watched as I racked up a really high score.

We eventually left the pier and who bumped into the Headteacher and his group going on! My group went rushing up and said excitedly, "Sir, Sir, we've just been on the pier and Barry got a really high score on the pinball." He looked at me and smiled as he disappeared into the games.

Later that night we were in the bar listening to the children via the intercoms and there was a lot of chatter. The Headteacher took the control and switched a switch which meant that he could talk to all the rooms at once. Then he spoke into the microphone and said, "This is mission control. Don't you think it is time you settled down to sleep?" The roar that went up could have been heard in Ventnor, as the kids suddenly realised that we had been monitoring their rooms all week! A number of rather embarrassed individuals spoke to me on the coach home and asked if I had heard them talking and telling jokes – although I said I had they didn't realise that we could only listen in to one room at a time.

I learnt a tremendous amount about taking youngsters away and I was to become a regular 'member of staff' on both residential and day trips – all in my own time of course. I ended up going on 17 residential trips over the years with various schools. We visited some fantastic areas including Aysgarth Falls in Yorkshire (six times), Capel Curig in Snowdonia, Edale on the Peak District, Wick Court Centre in Somerset, Malham in Yorkshire, Coombe Martin in Devon, Hexham in Northumberland, Ambleside in the Lake District (three times) and many other spectacular areas.

I have fond memories of these trips and many photographs to accompany those memories. Many of the landscape photographs are now in my exhibition of over 600 wildlife and landscape shots.

I was once asked to give a talk on nocturnal animals to a local primary school in Saffron Walden. I have a stuffed five year old badger called Burt that died in a road accident and I took him along. The talk was to a class of eight year old children and they were very interested as I went through the presentation. I began to talk about the badgers and explained that Burt had not used his Green Cross Code, which was why he died. A little hand went up at the front and said, "Mr Wright, does that mean that if I don't use the Green Cross Code, I will get stuffed like Burt?" The teachers looked at me and laughed as they left in a hurry – how do you answer that?!

As you have probably gathered schools were a very important part of my role as a rural bobby. I still do a lot of work in schools but now as a naturalist and wildlife consultant.

Part Two
Police and Wildlife

Introduction

I joined the force in 1973 having come from a farming/wildlife background. I had gained a lot of qualifications in agriculture and animal husbandry but was unable to pursue a career in the industry so I decided to opt for a change of direction and joined the 'Essex and Southend-on-Sea Joint Constabulary' - now Essex Police.

I soon became well known for my wildlife interests and a number of wildlife incidents were passed to me. My nickname soon became "The Wildlife Man", which eventually became the title of my first book. In the early years most of the wildlife incidents involved poaching, which is simply the illegal taking of game such as pheasant, partridge, hares and rabbits. Rabbits are a slightly grey area in that although they are not game under current legislation, they are a pest species. Deer also fell into the category of game but offences of taking deer were covered under the Deer Act.

Soon after moving to Thaxted in 1977 I became embroiled in an interesting case involving a badger sett and snares. A local farmer had placed running snares, which are not illegal at time of writing, but placing them over and around a badger sett is illegal. The Essex Assistant Chief Constable, Terry Rands, heard about this case and came out to see me. He took a personal interest and requested that I keep him updated on the case's progress. Eventually I had to inform him that we had lost the case on a technicality and he was very disappointed.

In the late 1980s Terry Rands was one of the first 'Police Wildlife Liaison Officers' (PWLO) in the country and was responsible for setting up a team of PWLOs in Essex. I was one of the first to be appointed amidst a mass of publicity and media coverage, including television.

I was not only known in the force for my wildlife interests but I soon became well known in the local community. I was regarded as an expert, though of course I am not. I began to get some interesting calls of which the following are just a few of the more amusing.

A Monster In The Garden

A call came into my office, one bright and sunny June morning, from a distraught lady in Thaxted. She was reporting a 'monster' in her garden and asked if I would come and remove it. She was so upset that she could not describe what the monster was. I was not on duty but was curious so I called on her. She showed me through her house to the kitchen, which had a door that led out into the back garden. She had barricaded the door to prevent the monster from coming in.

I helped remove the carpet and bits that she had put up against the door before I opened it – by then the lady was in the process of leaving the kitchen in a hurry. Nothing was immediately evident so I called to her and asked her where it was, thinking that whatever it was had escaped. She shouted back to me as she disappeared, "It's on the clothes' line post." I walked down the garden and found on the post a pair of privet hawk moths that were mating!

I managed to get a jam jar from the lady's kitchen and very gently scooped the amorous pair off the post and into the jar. They did not seem to be particularly perturbed by the intrusion; obviously their minds were otherwise engaged! The lady was very grateful when I explained to her what they were and that they were totally harmless. I left via an alley down the side of the house as there was no way she was going to let me into the house with the monster. I took the moths to a local nature reserve where I am a warden and gently placed them on the trunk of a large oak tree - they appeared to be untroubled by the move.

A year later, again in June, I received a call from the same lady, simply saying, "They are back." She thought that the same pair had returned but obviously they were not as a new generation emerges each year. I explained to the lady that this was not the same pair but what I found curious was that there were no food plants for their caterpillars either in the lady's or the neighbours' gardens. I did suggest to the lady that she might remove the post but she declined. Once again I gathered them up and took them down to the nature reserve.

The following year at exactly the same time I got the call with a loud voice, "Barry, they are back". This went on for a number of years and I could never understand why they chose that particular garden and post. Eventually the lady moved away and the new occupant took the post down.

A Vampire In The Bedroom

I answered the phone one evening from a distressed female in Saffron Walden reporting an eight foot 'vampire' in her bedroom. Again, I was not on duty but went over with my large fish pond net. As with the previous incident the lady had barricaded her bedroom door and I had to clear the barricade before going in. I did not really know what to expect and was quite relieved as I entered that there wasn't a man with fangs and a red lined cape standing waiting for me!

As I checked around the room I suddenly spotted the cause of her concern. There, hanging on the curtain, was a tiny pipistrelle bat. I very gently gathered it up and it was quite happy in my warm hand, moving its head from side to side. I opened the window and spread my hand out with the bat still in the palm. It shuffled forward to my fingertips and suddenly flew into the air before disappearing into the darkness. In fairness to the lady she had not actually seen the bat. She had half shell lights on the walls of her bedroom and as the bat flew through the lights its shadow on the ceiling was huge!

An Anaconda In A Pond

A few years ago a programme was featured on television about a South American biologist who was studying anaconda snakes. He was seen catching these huge snakes in the swamps, the snakes' preferred habitat. It was an interesting programme but I never thought much more about it until I received a phone call one morning.

A couple at Takeley, near Stansted Airport, were reporting what they thought was a huge anaconda in their pond. Their address placed them just behind Stansted airport, so I began to wonder if someone had tried to smuggle one in and it had escaped. I was not going to take any chances, so I loaded everything in my car that I thought I'd need to catch a huge snake. I rang my control and asked them to create an incident on the computer.

I attended the address with some trepidation and met the elderly couple who showed me through to the back garden. It was with some relief that I spotted the two metre circular pond and realised that the snake couldn't be that big. As I approached I suddenly saw the 'anaconda' basking on the edge of the pond. It was a large grass snake, about a metre long. These are the largest and the most common of our three native snakes and quite harmless. I went back to the couple and told them what it was. They were both terrified of snakes and asked me to remove it or kill it. I told them that I would catch it and take it away.

I returned to the pond and as I did so the snake slid into the water. I managed to catch it in my net and place it in a box. As the couple did not want to see it I carried it back through the house before releasing it on the banks of the River Chelmer, far away from the couple's house.

A Lion's Scratching Post

One evening I had just gone off duty when I received a call from a very anxious woman. She said, "Mr Wright, I have found a scratching post for a lion in ………… Wood" - I do not want to give the exact location of the wood for reasons which will become apparent. I arranged with the lady to meet her at the entrance to the wood the following morning, and she said, "But it might get me." I replied, "Don't worry, I'll be with you." I didn't know what I was going to do if it was a lion, all I had was my truncheon, although I did suspect I knew what it was.

We met up as arranged the following morning at the entrance to the wood. She was very nervous as we entered the wood along a footpath. We had walked quite a way into the wood, when she suddenly grabbed my arm and said, "There it is" and pointed to a young tree by the side of the path ahead of us. I went and examined the tree and it confirmed my suspicions. The deep scratches extended up the trunk from the base to a height of about a metre and there was a lot of grease on the trunk. I gently informed the lady that it was a scratching post of a badger, she was very relieved.

She then joined me and we had a look around for the sett, as I knew it would be nearby. Sure enough we soon found the large holes in the ground and the lady was delighted as we stood and looked down at them. But then something quite magical happened. No, we didn't see a badger, but I thought I heard a sound coming from one of the entrances, which we approached very quietly and leaned forward. From deep within the sett we could hear the sound of snoring! As we stood listening the lady was in tears, she was so thrilled. We eventually moved away quietly and as we walked back to the entrance the lady could not stop talking and asking questions about badgers, she was absolutely delighted and had forgotten all about the lion!

A Big Cat

Remaining on the subject of cats we regularly get 'big cat' sightings in Essex and normally the details end up on my desk. The reports ranged from black panthers to lions, cougars to leopards and lynx.

Now before I go on, I should point out that I do not doubt the integrity of anyone making these reports, but I am afraid that I do remain sceptical about the presence of these big cats. According to one big cat expert there are over 100 big cats running wild in Britain and they have been breeding in the wild for over 25 years (at the time of writing).

I base my 'doubting Thomas' attitude on two theories. Firstly, if these cats were as abundant as we are lead to believe we would have sightings reported every day, but we do not. Secondly, if these cats had been running free for as long as alleged then why (at the time of writing), have we never had a big cat killed on the roads or shot by a farmer or gamekeeper anywhere in the country? Every other form of animal falls victim to the roads from badgers to wild boar (A12 at Chelmsford) and deer to ostrich!

One morning a call came in that I was convinced would reveal evidence of a big cat. Big cat paw prints had been found in the mud on the edge of the village pond at Finchingfield. I was not on duty but could not miss this opportunity to see for myself, so I drove to the pond where I met up with the local bobby who was a friend of mine. He showed me to the point where the print was and, sure enough, there in the mud ahead of us was a deep print.

The mud all around it was flat and smooth, which made the print stand out even more. My colleague had requested the attendance of a Scenes of Crime Officer to take a plaster cast of the print, which was facing towards the water, only feet from it. There were no other prints present. Before saying anything I pondered how we only had one print. I had to say something, so I turned to my colleague and said, "Are we looking at a one legged lion?" He looked at me and we both burst out laughing, we had been well and truly had. The Scenes of Crime Officer was quickly cancelled and it took some explaining to the media who were soon on the scene. I was left to deal with them in my position as the newly appointed Force Wildlife Crime Officer (FWCO). Someone had played a clever practical joke, which the press thought was very amusing. Fortunately they didn't report on it, at my request, as I feared 'copycat' reports (excuse the pun).

I am convinced that one day I will be proved wrong and a big cat will turn up somewhere, but at the time of writing I remain unconvinced of the presence of wild big cats in Britain.

An Animal With An Ear For Music

Thaxted Church is a very large church and is well known for its fine acoustics; many concerts are held within this wonderful building, throughout the year.

One year I was advised by my Inspector that a military band were appearing at the Church in a few weeks' time and I would be required for security duties with my friend, and special officer, Dave Kinnley.

On the day the band were due to play Dave and I came on duty at midday, just as the dog search team arrived at my office. After a cup of tea we all attended the church and the labradors were put to work sniffing for explosives. An extensive search was commenced and we left them to it.

We returned when the 'exploding dogs' had finished and the church was then sealed until the band and the audience began to arrive. At that time the Inspector arrived to check that all was going well. As was his manner, he looked immaculate, his uniform pristine. In the church he had a look around and asked if the boiler room in the basement had been checked. I did not know as I had not been present when the exploding dogs were doing their stuff, so he decided to go down and check. I did warn him that it was pretty dirty down there but he insisted on going down himself.

We removed the grill and down he went. I offered to hold his cap but he kept it on. He was gone for ages and I became a little concerned. Suddenly a cap appeared from the basement, covered in cobwebs and dust. The Inspector rose out of the ground like an apparition covered from head to foot in dust and cobwebs. He did not look at all happy and the phrase 'I told you so' came to mind. He left via a side door and we did not see him again that night.

The band was soon in place and the Church was filling up. I had been told that this concert had been sold out for weeks and soon the crowds were pouring in. The band master spoke to Dave and myself and advised us that the second half of the evening was going to be taken up with Tchaikovsky's 1812 Overture. The cannon fire at the end was going to be simulated by the firing of a number of rifles with blank ammunition.

Dave and I positioned ourselves behind the stage where the band was, which left us under the tall spire and the belfry. We were in a prime position to enjoy the music and we did. With the first half and the interval over we settled down to the 1812, one of my favourite pieces of music. Dave leaned forward to me with a smile on his face and said, "Watch what happens when the rifles are fired." I didn't quite understand what he meant.

There were an estimated 1300 people in the church and they were facing us. We were out of sight behind the band. As the overture reached the final crescendo, I braced myself for the rifles that were going to be fired by a number of soldiers standing near the stage. Suddenly there was an ear splitting bang as the first of the volleys rang out. Almost immediately, and to my utter surprise, a huge black ball fell out of the belfry and a number of tiny pipistrelle bats began flying around the Church. I am not exaggerating when I say that there must have been in excess of 400.

All the audience looked up at the bats that were flying above their heads and many placed their programmes over their heads to protect them from these tiny mammals. If only I had had my camera I could have got a lovely shot. Dave looked at me, smiled and winked. Many faces in the audience were looking very nervous as their heads bobbed and the bats swooped.

What was really surprising was that as quickly as the bats appeared they all disappeared again through a tiny gap above the south porch of the Church. Slowly the programmes were lowered from the audience's heads.

With the concert over, the band were all talking about the bats and the reaction of the audience. Even the organisers of the concerts were asking about the bats. One lady from the audience came up to me and said, "Who released those nasty creatures? I hope that you will be speaking to them, it was a stupid thing to do, and spoiled the concert for me." I tried to explain that they had come out of the belfry but I don't think she believed me; she went off in a huff.

An Unusual Excuse For Being Late For Work

Early one morning I was eating breakfast with Pat when we heard a loud cacophony coming from the driveway along the side of the house. We went out to investigate and found a grey squirrel on the drive in front of my car. Closer examination revealed a second (baby) squirrel, underneath the car. I was about to leave for work so I grabbed my coat and walked towards the car.

The adult scolded me and ran up and along the garden fence. The baby just sat there until I tried to get it to move then, to my amazement, it jumped up into the engine compartment. The adult had moved towards me along the fence, still scolding me. I lifted the bonnet of the car to scare the baby out but I couldn't see it anywhere. We both searched the engine and finally Pat spotted its tail sticking out from behind a metal plate that held the engine in place. I knew that if I started the engine it would probably kill the little creature but how were we going to get it out?

We pondered the problem while I rang Dunmow Police Station and informed them that I was going to be late - I don't think they believed me when I told them why! Pat fetched a long bamboo cane and I crawled under the car to get the angle with the cane. The baby squirrel would not move, in spite of my prodding, so we fetched a length of strong wire to see if I could get behind it. Eventually, after a lot of effort and cursing, the baby jumped out and sat on the concrete close to my head with the adult going berserk on the fence. As I slid out from under the car the baby suddenly scuttled away and up the fence to join its parent.

I eventually arrived at work almost an hour late and was talking to the Sergeant in the front office when the Inspector came down from his office. He looked at me, and said with a smile, "I've heard of some excuses in my time for being late, but a squirrel in the engine takes the cake!" I gave up trying to explain.

A Little Brown Box

One morning I came on duty at 09:00 and immediately received a call from Irene Munro, the front office clerk at Dunmow Police Station. A little brown box had been left outside the front door of the station when she opened up that morning with a note on top stating 'Mother killed in road accident.' Apparently inside were six tiny ducklings and I had been requested to attend the office and collect them.

I attended and came into the station via the back door. As I walked through I could hear a lot of loud squawking coming from the cell - Dunmow only had one cell in the old police station. I went through to the front office and spoke to Irene who had placed the box into the empty cell. I went to the cell and found that all the occupants of the box, six day-old Mallard ducklings, were out and running around the floor squawking, one in particular was really loud. I managed to gather them all up and put them back into the box. As I carried the box through to the front office there was still a lot of noise coming from within.

What I hadn't realised was that it was 'press day'. This is when local reporters come in to be briefed by the Inspector on any incidents or occurrences that the media may be able to assist us with or may be interested in. When they saw me holding the box they had their story! I had to do a photo session with them in the rear car park and they loved it, a human interest story on wildlife.

When we had finished I carefully placed the box in the car and drove off, the ducklings still as noisy as ever. As I drove down the main road the noisiest of the ducklings managed to escape from the box and ended up stuck under the front passenger seat of the police car. I had to pull over and extricate the miscreant from under the seat and return it to the box.

I took the ducklings to an animal sanctuary that I used from time to time. They were placed into an intensive care unit and the lady who ran the sanctuary acted as a surrogate mother to them. Despite the trauma that the ducklings had experienced in losing their mum and being 'arrested' and placed in a cell, they all survived. The photograph shows two of the ducklings ten days later and, yes, one did leave me with a parting gift on my shirt - something my wife is quite used to! All the ducklings survived and were eventually released in a local wildlife park.

A Very Lucky Yorkshire Terrier

Although I did not actually witness this incident I was involved in the subsequent aftermath. One sunny morning in midsummer a little old lady was walking her Yorkshire Terrier across the village green not far from my house.

The dog was on an extending lead, which may have saved its life. The old lady was enjoying her stroll across the green and the tiny dog was sniffing around, oblivious of what was going to happen next.

Suddenly there was a whoosh past the lady's head, which startled her. Almost immediately the terrier disappeared into the air in the talons of a huge owl. Within seconds the dog's lead had fully extended and the startled, desperate lady yanked the lead, which appeared to surprise the bird. The sudden jerk caused it to open its talons and the bird dropped its prey. The hapless dog fell, its fall cushioned by the soft ground and the fairly long grass.

The lady rushed over, gathered up the dog and tucked it under her arm before rushing for a shelter on the edge of the green, but the huge predator had not finished with the dog. It swung around and swooped low and fast towards the terrified lady with her dog. The lady reached the shelter and the bird gave up the attack before flying over the shelter into a nearby tree. A passing postman had witnessed the attacks and rushed over to the lady who was very shaken.

It was at this point that I got a call; I was not on duty at the time but offered to help. I suspected that the owl may have escaped from a private collector, although I could find no trace of any reported loss. From the description to my control from the postman it sounded like a European Eagle Owl, one of the largest birds of prey in Europe with a wing span of 1.7m and the largest owl in the world. When I arrived the lady had been taken to a nearby house and given a cup of tea. I examined the dog, which despite its experience, was not badly hurt though it did have some deep puncture marks from the talons. The distance between these puncture marks more or less confirmed my suspicions that it was an Eagle Owl.

I offered to take the lady and the dog to a local vet for the dog to be checked over. It was given the all clear and some cream to rub into the wounds. I took the lady and the dog to her home, and then went looking for the miscreant bird but there was no sign of it near the green; even a huge bird like this can easily disappear. I eventually gave up the search and just hoped it didn't attack any other dog or cat.

The following day a report came in that a European Eagle Owl had escaped from an aviary in Saffron Walden and, almost at the same time, another report came in of a huge owl sitting on a roof of a house near to where yesterday's attack had occurred. I met the owl's owner and we attended the last reported sighting of his bird. We didn't have to look very far as a group of people were standing looking up at a roof where the bird sat looking down.

The owner placed a leather gauntlet on his hand and showed the bird a dead day-old chick; within a short space of time the bird was on his gloved fist, tucking into the dead chick, obviously hungry. The bird looked impressive as it sat on his fist and he placed it on a special perch in the back of his car then left. The owl's owner sent a bunch of flowers to the lady by way of an apology.

These owls are probably the most formidable bird of prey that I have ever had the privilege to look after and we bred them at Jersey Zoo in the 1960s.

The Tenacity Of A Pair Of Blackbirds.

One spring morning I received a phone call from a Thaxted resident that resulted in one of the most fascinating incidents involving a pair of blackbirds. The story so far went like this: a pair of blackbirds had built a nest in the engine of a car, which was being used daily to take some children to a school in Cambridge, some 25 miles from Thaxted.

The birds were very patient and waited for the car to return before continuing building the nest. They gained access to the engine via a front wheel arch. The owners thought that the birds would abandon the nest, but the birds had other ideas. The hen bird laid four eggs in the nest and, every morning when the children got into the car and slammed their doors, the hen would hop out and up onto the fence where she watched the car and her precious clutch disappear up the road. The car was gone for over an hour but, as soon as the car returned, the bird would hop back under the bonnet. I can only assume that the heat of the engine kept the eggs warm.

This routine continued for some days until one morning four baby blackbirds appeared in the nest. It was at this point that the couple rang me and I took my camera down; I found the story quite intriguing. Fortunately the husband of the car owner had mentioned this unusual nest site to his firm of accountants in London and they were so fascinated that they hired a car for his wife to use while the young birds grew and fledged the nest, at which point the nest could be removed. There was also a real fire risk, as the outside of the nest was dead grass and the nest itself was very close to the battery!

All four chicks successfully fledged the nest, and this just goes to show the tenacity of birds.

Whisky Galore

This is another story about a Yorkshire Terrier that got me into a bit of trouble. It all began one Sunday lunchtime when I was off duty and about to eat my Sunday roast. Someone knocked at the office door and I went through to find a man standing at the door holding three Yorkshire terriers in his arms. I invited him in and he told me that he had just found one of the dogs trotting along a road near Thaxted. Now the normal procedure is to take the dog, complete a load of paperwork and send the dog to the dog pound; or alternatively to fill in another form for the finder to retain the dog if they wished.

The gentleman stated that he would be more than happy to look after the little dog, which seemed to be content with his dogs. As this was allowed I took down all his details. The dog he had found had no collar and this was way before the days of micro chipping. Therefore, the problem was resolved - everyone was happy including the dog. After the appropriate paperwork had been completed the man left the office.

I phoned Saffron Walden Police Station and an entry was made in the Found Dog Register, but no Yorkshire Terriers had been reported missing. As the gentleman left he commented, "I am going away for a few days and the dogs will be with me", which did not really register with me. I thought that was the end of the matter.

On Monday morning at 09:00 I was off duty when I received a phone call from a very angry lady who was the owner of the found dog. She had been given the details of the gentleman who was looking after her dog and had rung him, only to discover that her dog was safe and well, but was in Scotland! The comment from the gentleman as he had left my office now had new significance, why had I not asked him where he was going? Incidentally, this was the same question asked by the duty Inspector later the same day. The lady was making arrangements to fly up to Scotland to retrieve her dog with the intention of sending the bill to the police - I felt a formal complaint coming on here.

The duty Inspector contacted me and was not happy at all. Later that day the Divisional Commander's secretary rang me to say that he was on his way over to see me; I was for the high jump, albeit that I had followed procedures correctly. If only I had asked the man where he was going!

The Chief Superintendent arrived and I showed him in, gave him a cup of tea and explained what had happened. He burst out laughing, which was a great relief to me, and said, "You do realise that we will probably have to pay for this dog's holiday," and laughed. He did however say that the owner of the dog was not going to Scotland after all as the man with her dog was on his way back; that was quite a relief. As he left he said, "Only you could send a found dog to Scotland for a holiday, consider yourself reprimanded," and laughed all the way back to his car.

Well I had ridden the storm and I thought that was the end of the matter but somehow the local media got to hear about the story and it made front page on all the local papers along with pictures of the dog reunited with its owner. One headline read, 'Whiskey Galore!' I was the butt of a lot of jokes for quite a while.

An Unusual Chimney Sweep?

I was forever having injured or baby owls brought around to me to care for, though I don't really know why. I was always annoyed to find boxes left outside the house with baby owls inside. People have a compunction to pick up baby birds and take them away when really they should be left for the parents to rear them - as I always say, "Let nature take its course."

One of the problems with hand-rearing any birds, and owls in particular, is that once they are of an age where they can be released back into the wild, difficulties are then experienced in that we can not teach them to hunt for food or how to establish a territory, which is particularly important with owls. The usual result is death by starvation or a life in captivity, which in my view is cruel and unnecessary.

Now, having pontificated about wild birds being brought into captivity, I have had quite a bit of success in caring for injured owls and returning (hacking) them back into the wild. The next two stories are about birds that I had some success with.

Early one December morning I received a phone call from a local farmer who informed me that he had managed to rescue an adult Tawny Owl from his chimney, where it had been trapped for seven days! The bird was very weak and close to death; he asked if I could have a look at it. I called on the farmer who was a friend and he showed me the bird that was sitting hunched up in the corner of a cardboard box. I told him that I would try but it didn't look promising.

Back at home Pat and I examined the bird but there did not appear to be any obvious injuries. The bird was obviously very weak and it was important to get some food inside it. Fortunately we keep a supply of dead rats, mice, birds and day-old chicks in the bottom drawer of our freezer in the kitchen, especially for this eventually. I located a nice, juicy mouse and defrosted it in the microwave.

An owl like this one who we nicknamed 'Ollie' (not very original, I know), will not normally take dead food, especially when in captivity, so force-feeding is required, which is not easy with owls. The technique is to hold the food in one hand, and open the beak with the finger and thumb of the other hand, which sounds easy until you try.

Although Ollie was weak, he was able to resist my attempts to begin with, but with a lot of perseverance the mouse was in his huge mouth and with a little friendly persuasion Ollie swallowed. It was quite a relief to see the tail disappear and we placed him back in his box to quietly digest his meal. Our downstairs toilet doubles as an aviary/hospital, but of course we have to make sure that the toilet lid is kept down!

It is often shock that kills birds within 24 hours of coming into captivity, so it was with some relief that when we opened the box the following morning Ollie was sitting upright and looking quite perky. I left the lid of the box open but he was happy to remain in there for he was still too weak to fly.

The following evening I gave Ollie another mouse - he still resisted my efforts to open his beak but without the vigour from the previous night. The next morning Ollie was out of the box and had managed to get up onto a shelf full of shoes above the toilet, obviously his strength was returning.

The next evening I got him down from the shelf and fed him a rat. He did not resist but as I placed the rat in his open mouth, his claw slowly came up and his talon lodged in my thumb, which was extremely painful. Owl's talons are extremely sharp for obvious reasons and although the wound remained painful for a few days, it was satisfying that Ollie was on the mend and his spirit was returning.

We fed Ollie up for ten days and this gave the farmer time to place some wire mesh over the chimney pot to avoid a repetition of the incident. One evening Ollie was placed back in his box, which he didn't take to kindly to. We drove to the farm where he had joined the ranks of chimney sweeps and met up with the farmer who was delighted that we had been able to save him from his near-death experience. I carried the box around the back of the farm house and placed it down on to the grass before opening the lid. Ollie looked out into the darkness and sat there for a moment before rising out of the box on silent wings. Within seconds he had disappeared into the darkness, a lovely moment for Pat and I. As I reached down to pick up Ollie's box we heard a loud hoot from the direction that he had flown off, was he saying thank you?

A Toad's Green Cross Code

During spring amphibians come out of their hibernation and begin the trek back to the ponds, normally where they were born, to breed. This will often involve crossing roads where their mortality rate can be high. People will often help the frogs and toads across the road by gathering them up into a bucket and carrying them across the road before emptying them out.

One particular lady in a local village used to spend almost two weeks every spring helping toads cross the road. Her actions must have helped the toads because their population increased dramatically, to the point where the lady could not cope with the numbers, and had to she enlist the help of the local Cub Scout pack. Their leader agreed, saying it could be part of the boys' Conservation badge.

One evening I received a complaint from a motorist expressing concern that the boys were in uniform and could not be seen by motorists in the unlit road. I went over and spoke to the lady and the cub leader and suggested they all wear high visibility coats so they could be seen clearly. 'Police Slow' signs were placed out to slow the traffic down, but fortunately the road was not a main road.

A few nights later I received a further complaint that buckets of toads were being taken away to be put in other ponds in the village. Unfortunately this was not very helpful for the toads as they would still try and return to their birth place. I mentioned this to the lady and she stopped the practice immediately.

The lady and a team of volunteers continued assisting the toads for many years with no further problems and there continues to be a very healthy amphibian population in this village.

A Scorpion

Early one morning at Braintree Police Station, the office clerk was on the phone when a young woman rushed up to the public counter carrying a small brown box that was sealed up. She shouted through the glass panel, "I found this in a box of peaches I bought at a car boot sale at Witham," then left the box on the counter with no other details.

The clerk finished her phone call and wandered over to the counter, slid the security glass divide across, and took the box. She opened it and, according to witnesses, gave out a loud scream, jumped back and dropped the box - inside was a large brown scorpion. A PC standing nearby rushed over and managed to gather up the creature before it had time to run off - they can move amazingly fast. It was returned to its box, which was then resealed. Unfortunately, we had no idea who the lady was that had brought it in.

I was not on duty at the time but I got a call and went over to see what I could do. What do you do with a live and potentially dangerous insect? The golden rule with scorpions (one that I learnt at Jersey Zoo) is that the larger the pincers, the less dangerous the venom. After looking at it and discovering that it did in fact have large pincers, I was still not going to take any chances with it and sealed the box securely. I made a number of calls, including one to

London Zoo, but no-one wanted it. Eventually it was taken in by Colchester Zoo, and an RSPCA Inspector collected it from me and took it over there. I was quite relieved to see it go!

A Kestrel, A Fox Hunt,
A Rabbit And A Stoat

Now, you may be wondering how all these creatures feature in a story but all will be revealed! Early one morning I was covering a Wednesday meet of the Essex Fox Hunt at the Red Lion Public House at Great Sampford, which was on my beat. We used to cover these meets to prevent trouble between members of the hunt and the antis, or saboteurs, although we rarely had trouble at the weekday meets, problems usually happened at the Saturday meets.

The hunt rode off through the village and out into the country. There were no antis and I remained with the hunt for about an hour. I was about to leave when a local farmer came up to me carrying a box. Inside was a beautiful female kestrel that was unable to fly although her wings seemed to be undamaged. The farmer had found it under some high voltage power lines and he believed that the bird had hit them. I took the bird home and rang a vet friend of mine who said he would call in at midday when passing.

The vet examined the bird and reported that the bird had a fractured sternum. As this held the flight muscles the bird could not fly. He said it would be unlikely to survive the shock but I could try. The bird was placed in a small aviary I had in the back garden and a flat tree stump log was placed in there for a perch. The bird wasted no time in jumping up onto the low perch and sat there, surveying her surroundings. I took a dead mouse from the freezer, thawed it out in the microwave and placed it in the aviary near the bird.

As I walked away I watched the kestrel and, to my total surprise, when I turned around the bird had dragged the mouse up onto the perch and was feeding well. I can not describe the feeling of satisfaction, as an injured creature starts to feed for itself. May be there was a chance that this bird would survive, despite the vet's scepticism. The bird was obviously very hungry and I pondered just how long she had been injured. I named her Kes, another original name!

The following morning I raced down at day break to see if she was still alive and she was. She looked quite perky on her perch and I gave her another mouse. Again within a short space of time she was tucking in. It was a relief that I was not going to have to force feed her - owls are bad enough but a kestrel was going to be a whole new ball game. Days went by and my food store of mice was rapidly diminishing, I was going to need to find some more dead animals.

One morning I gave Kes my last mouse and this meant that I needed to look for some more food. I did have some dead day-old chicks in the freezer but I didn't think she would like them, however, luck was on my side - or so I thought.

I was driving through the village of Great Sampford to do an enquiry in the next village. As I was leaving the village, on the brow of a hill, I saw a dead rabbit lying in the middle of the road. I assumed that it was a road casualty so I stopped the car and got out to pick up the corpse, which was going to be a good food supply for Kes. As I approached I suddenly spotted something wrapped around the rabbit. My initial reaction was that it was a snake, but given the time of year, it couldn't be. As I got closer I could see that it was a stoat - it had the rabbit by the throat and had wrapped itself around the hapless animal. The stoat looked at me but would not let go of its prey. I went back to the police car to fetch my truncheon to try and prod the stoat away.

As I approached, the stoat let go of the dead rabbit and ran off into the grass verge. I picked up the rabbit and placed it in the back of the police car. As I got in I noticed the stoat reappear from the verge and, as I shut the door, the animal ran over to the car and suddenly sat up and looked at me. To my amazement it then began to run around the car, frequently stopping and sitting bolt upright, looking at the car. I could only assume that it had watched me place its kill in the car and it wanted it back, but my need was greater!

I started the engine and drove off but as I looked in the rear view mirror I could see the stoat sitting bolt upright in the middle of the road looking towards me; I must admit that I felt a little sorry for it. I quickly completed my enquiry and returned along the stretch of road where the stoat had been. To my astonishment it was still there searching up and down the side of the road where I had parked. The rabbit lasted Kes quite a while as I fed it to her in pieces.

As the weeks went by her strength returned and she began to open her wings. Her right wing had lost one of its primary feathers in the accident but it would not affect her flying. As the first signs of spring began with some warm days, Kes began to call from her aviary and was flying up and down in an excited manner - I decided that it might be the right time for her to be hacked back to the wild.

One beautiful, warm, sunny morning in late March, the time had come for Kes to go. I gave her a mouse early on as it was important that she went out with a full crop. The aviary was carried onto the waste ground at the rear of police house and I opened the door at the top. Kes looked up, cocked her head to one side, then flew up and out of the aviary and rose into the blue sky with ease. The gap in her wing where the feather was missing did not appear to be bothering her. It was a lovely moment, I was happy that she was returning to the wild but this feeling was tinged with a little sadness, as I had become very attached to her. She disappeared over a hedge and was gone.

I looked out for her for the rest of the day but she had gone, or so I thought. The following morning I looked out of my bedroom window and, to my utter surprise, there was Kes hovering high in the sky above the rough grass behind the house – she was searching the ground. Suddenly she folded her wings and dropped fast into the grass only to reappear shortly after with a rodent in her talons. The fact that she was hunting was a great relief to me. For a long time after this Kes could be seen hunting this rough area which was full of rodents and insects, her return to the wild had been one hundred percent successful and I was very pleased, though I don't think the stoat was!

A Little Cottage With A Big Dog

Dogs have always been the bane of police officers' lives, whether a stray dog, a dangerous dog, a noisy dog or a dog worrying livestock, they are always a problem. Some, if not all, local authorities employ dog or animal wardens, but it seemed to be the case that when a problem occurred they were not on duty, like police officers I suppose!

One morning I came on duty at 09:00 and the phone rang straight away. It was Dunmow Police who wanted me to call at a small cottage in a nearby village within the Dunmow section. I was to speak to a lady about keeping her dog under control when out walking it – a fairly simple job I thought, so I agreed to do it.

I drove out to the small, thatched cottage and parked outside. As I approached the cottage I noticed a large duvet hanging out of an upstairs window, which I didn't see the significance of at the time.

I knocked on the front door which had low leaded windows either side. I immediately heard a really deep loud, "Wow, wow, wow, wow," from within - it was obviously a very large dog. I waited but no-one came to the door so I knocked again. The bark had got nearer and was to the left of the door. I looked through the low window and initially couldn't see anything, but the cold realisation came over me that I was looking through the front legs of a dog!

I stepped back from the window but curiosity got the better of me and I looked again. The front legs of the beast were leaning against the wall above the window. Suddenly a huge head appeared between the legs and my heart missed a beat. The head filled the entire window and the mouth of the dog went right across his face. I am certain that the entire window vibrated as the dog barked against the glass.

I then heard a voice above the barking, asking me to wait. All went quiet as the dog disappeared from the window. I don't mind saying that I was rather nervous as I heard the door opening. A face appeared around the corner of the door and when she saw that I was in uniform the door opened. A very tiny lady appeared holding on to what I can only say was a huge, monster of a dog on a lead. It was a sandy brown coloured English Bull Mastiff. When it saw me it rushed out pulling the woman with it. The lady shouted, "It's okay, he is quite friendly," but I wasn't so sure. The dog sniffed my uniform trousers and, suddenly without warning, jumped up and rested its front paws on my shoulders! Once again I was eyeball to eyeball with the dog. He was the biggest dog I had ever seen, and very heavy. Fortunately he did turn out to be friendly, which was just as well really as he started licking my face - I didn't argue with him. I was eventually let into the house, but the dog named Buster continued to pay a lot of attention to my trousers, I believe he could smell my dogs which were both bitches.

I explained to the lady that complaints had been made about Buster not being kept under control when she was out walking him. She said that she found it very difficult to hold him on his lead when other dogs were around, and he also had an affinity to cats. If Buster ran off she would hold on tight to the lead but would end up flying through the air like a cartoon character - her analogy not mine, but it painted an interesting picture. I advised her that she must keep him under control otherwise she could end up in court.

I sat and had a cup of tea with the lady and could hear another dog barking in another room. Eventually I was introduced to a second dog, a big Rottweiller - Buster made this second dog look like a terrier. I then enquired about the duvet hanging out of the bedroom window and was advised that it was Buster's bed. He and the other dog slept in the bedroom with the lady, who lived on her own. It would be a brave, or stupid, burglar to break into that cottage! We had no further complaints.

A Determined Woodpecker

Living where we are, we are surrounded by open countryside and woodlands, perfect for walking the dogs. One morning I was out nice and early across the fields with Cassie and Pat's black Labrador, Chela. It was a beautiful spring day and skylarks were high in the clear blue sky, singing their little hearts out, before dropping like stones into the fields.

As we approached one of the woods, known as Terriers' Wood, I could see men working. A large lorry was unloading a number of long wooden telegraph poles at the edge of the wood. Curiosity got the better of me and, as we passed the lorry, I enquired as to what was happening. I was informed that the electricity cables that ran through the wood were going to be diverted around the wood and over the next few days the poles were to be put up. One morning I noticed a Greater Spotted Woodpecker on one of the poles, drumming towards the top, which I assumed was a territorial drumming.

A few days later I received a phone call from the electricity board, requesting my attendance at the site where the poles were being erected. To my surprise, I was taken to the pole that I had seen the woodpecker drumming onto and, there, towards the top, was a hole right through the pole! As we stood there the female bird came out and it was then apparent that she had not only drilled straight through the pole, but had dug down into the pole as well. I could not understand why she had decided to nest in this extremely hard, wooden pole when there were plenty of nest sites within the mature oak wood nearby. The contractors wanted to bring the pole down and replace it but I advised them that as a nest in use it was protected by law and that they would have to wait until the birds fledged the nest. The workmen were not very happy but agreed to comply. Six weeks later the nest was vacated when the adult pair had successfully raised and fledged four offspring who spent their early days in the wood. The pole was brought down and replaced with a new one and, to prevent this problem arising again, the contractors placed metal jackets around all the poles, from top to bottom, in the vicinity of the wood. The woodpeckers are now flying around with bent beaks!

Noisy Owls!

One morning I was contacted by the animal warden for my local district council. He asked me if I could assist him with a complaint from residents regarding some noisy owls owned by a couple in the village. I had not dealt with a complaint of this nature before but I agreed to assist.

We met at his office and, before we left to see the owl's owner, he played me a tape recording made by one of the neighbours of the owls through the night - the noise was tremendous and continued for a long time.

We then left the office and soon arrived at the house, which was in the middle of an estate. The man was expecting us and invited us in, taking us through to his back garden. He had a number of huge aviaries running down one side of the garden housing two Barn Owls in one and two in another. They were separated by a larger aviary containing a pair of beautiful Snowy Owls. It transpired that the guilty parties were the Barn Owls. It was the beginning of the breeding season and the Barn Owls were swearing at each other through the aviary that separated them.

We didn't need to play the tape to the owner as he accepted that he had a problem that needed to be resolved.

He felt that the neighbours were fully justified in their complaint.

We had a cup of tea with him and his wife and it soon became apparent to us that this couple were owl enthusiasts as everything in the house had owls on it. There were owl pictures everywhere and owl plates on the wall. The curtains had owls on them, the wallpaper in the sitting room had owls on, even the lampshades and the mugs that we were drinking our tea from had owls on. I do not think that I have ever met a couple that were quite so enthusiastic about these beautiful birds. I did look after a number of owls at Jersey Zoo whilst I was there and I must admit that they are one of my favourites.

After a brief discussion the man agreed to sell one of the pairs of barn owls but did say that he would be replacing them with another species of owl. The problem was resolved, both for the remaining pair that could now get on and breed, and for the neighbours.

An Owl With Attitude

It was a cold and frosty morning a few days before Christmas when my wife Pat took a call from a gentleman in a nearby village claiming that he had a Snowy Owl in his garden and it appeared to be very weak. Now, Snowy Owls are not native to this country although they will sometimes appear in the far north, so I was very interested. I was not on duty but curiosity got the better of me and I decided to call on the gentleman to see what exactly he had got.

I was shown into the back garden of the house where, to my amazement, under an apple tree on the lawn sat a female Snowy Owl. Because of the feathered legs and feet I could not see if the bird had any metal rings on. I had a net with me and slowly approached the bird, her bright yellow eyes glaring at me, and as I got nearer she began to hiss loudly - she may have been weak but she defended herself admirably. I dropped the net over her and gathered her up; surprisingly she did not struggle.

I took her back to the car, holding onto her firmly and at the car I carefully removed her from the netting with hardly any struggling. This, unfortunately, was my undoing for I got complacent. As I lowered her into a box I had in the car, she suddenly struck out viciously with her needle sharp 1½" long talons, one of which pierced through my police issue leather gloves and went right through the side of my wrist, boy that hurt! It bled and bled. I removed the talon with some difficulty as she tried to strike out again and again. Eventually the blood-stained talon was out and I closed the lid on those glaring yellow eyes.

I cleaned the wound as best I could at the gentleman's house before returning home with the bird. I carefully placed her in a large wooden holding box with bars on the front. Although she was still glaring at me, she very quickly devoured a dead day-old chick that I offered her.

I circulated the find on the Police computer and was soon contacted by the bird's owner who lived 10 miles away. It had escaped as he was feeding it. Bird and owner were re-united.

An Unusual Pet

One morning I received a report from control of a wildlife job at Takeley. I called on the informant, a very dear old lady, and had a cup of tea with her as she recited her story. She was complaining that her neighbour was shooting the garden birds in his garden - she claimed that it was one bird about every four weeks and the significance of the time gap became apparent later. I explained that I needed a little more evidence than just her allegation, although I did not doubt her word, and she fully understood. I also explained that the Chief Constable would not sanction me sitting in her lounge for four weeks waiting for the next bird to be shot. She laughed and agreed. I left her my card and asked her to ring me when it happened again.

Over the next few days I made some enquiries about the man who lived on his own in the house next to the old lady, but nothing was known about him. About a week after I had seen the lady, she rang me one morning when I was off duty and reported that her neighbour had just shot a blackbird which had landed in her garden. The man had called on her requesting to retrieve the bird but she had refused. When I came on duty I called on the lady. The dead bird was on her patio and I took some photos for evidence. I took a quick statement from the lady who thought it was all very exciting, finished my cup of tea and left to call on the neighbour.

I knocked at the door and eventually the door was opened by a huge man whose build filled the door in all directions. After a long time in the force, one learns to call these people "Sir", but it didn't work. As soon as he saw me he tried to shut the door but I already had my foot in the way! However, as soon as I mentioned that I was a Wildlife Officer, his attitude changed and he said, "Come in mate, sorry about that, I fell against the door. Come in and have a cup of tea and a piece of Dundee cake." As I entered his sitting room it became apparent why he was shooting one garden bird every four weeks. There, in a vivarium which extended along one wall of the room, was a huge snake that I was soon to learn was a three metre long Reticulated Python. We had had one called 'Retic' which was seven metres long at Jersey Zoo. Snakes will normally only feed very sporadically hence the gap between shooting the birds.

He accepted that he was doing wrong and after finishing my cake and a cup of tea I reported him for shooting the birds, though he was not very happy when I seized his gun. He eventually appeared before Dunmow Magistrates' Court where he pleaded guilty to killing protected birds. He was fined £200 with £50 costs and a destruction order was put on his gun. Fortunately he was not banned from keeping the snake as I had visions of trying to find a home for a three metre snake that would eventually grow into a huge and potentially dangerous creature. The snake is now fed on dead day-old chicks.

'Operation Tortoise'

Soon after being appointed as one of the first Wildlife Liaison Officers in the force, I became involved with a Sergeant and a number of officers in an operation code named 'Operation Tortoise'. The operation had come about as a result of a massive increase in incidents of illegal hare coursing in the north-west area of the county, with its rolling hills and huge fields. It wasn't just the coursing incidents but it was the assaults, damage, threats and thefts that were associated with some of the people involved in this activity when they were challenged by aggrieved landowners and gamekeepers. A number of landowners had got together and approached the Essex Chief Constable at the time, Mr John Burrow, asking for assistance and police support in dealing with these incidents which were regularly occurring on Sundays between September and March every year.

For those of you who might not know what hare coursing is, basically it is the running of a pair of greyhounds or lurchers on a hare when bets, some quite big, are placed on which dog gets nearest to the hare before the dogs 'burn out'. These dogs normally have a turn of speed for 450 to 500 metres. A hare can run flat out for a lot further. Some bets will be placed on which hound makes the hare turn the most. The coursers will prefer large, open fields as these types of dogs hunt by sight alone. From a legal point of view, when Operation Tortoise was set up hare coursing was not illegal if a landowner had given permission for the coursers to go on the land and it was not on a Sunday (no game can be taken on a Sunday except fish). In February 2005 the Hunting with Hounds Act came in, which not only banned fox hunting but also hare coursing.

When the operation was set up, a number of meetings were held with the landowners and gamekeepers, as we were going to work closely with them especially since we had no four wheeled drive vehicles apart from the Traffic

Department on the motorway. The plan, therefore, was to patrol with the keepers and landowners in their vehicles using backpack police radios and the keepers' CB radios, which were all the rage at that time. I had a CB base station in my office at Thaxted and my handle, or call sign, was "Fuzzy Bear". When I was on the radio in the office I was known as "Fuzzy Bear in the Bear Cage", but that is another story! Of course this was before the days of mobile phones.

Operation Tortoise began and immediately became a very successful operation. It soon attracted the attentions of both local and national media and a number of television companies, including a French network, came out with us to film and record our activities; there was plenty for them to see.

I recall a reporter for Radio 4 coming out with us one Sunday morning. He was sitting in the back of a brand new police Land Rover that I was driving. He was recording interviews with us and planned to record any activities that might arise. During an interview with me a call went up for coursers in the middle of a field near to where we were. We drove off and entered the field through a gap in the hedge before racing across the stubble field. The poor reporter was bouncing around on the back seat and soon terminated the interview. We saw two coursers who ran off when they saw us but we were soon onto them.

My colleague, Trevor Bailey, and I spoke to the men and the reporter tried to record the conversation, but I had to stop him as this could jeopardise any future prosecution. On checking the men's identities on the Police National Computer (PNC), it was revealed that one of the men was wanted by Thames Valley Police for supplying drugs. We detained him and placed him in the back of the Land Rover as back-up had arrived. The other man and the dogs were placed in another Police vehicle. The reporter tried to interview the detained man in my vehicle but he was told to go away, or words to that effect! The men and their dogs were taken to Saffron Walden Police Station where Thames Valley Police later collected man wanted by them. We took the reporter back out and dealt with two more groups of coursers - the reporter had plenty of material and a sore head from hitting his head on the roof of the Land Rover!

On another occasion a large group of coursers were seen in a huge field adjacent to the M11 motorway. They were strung out in a long line with their hounds on leads. Two of the coursers were walking ahead of the main group and from our position we could just see them through the mist. Two vehicles were sent to challenge them while we, along with another vehicle, were sent to try and intercept them if they ran off, which they did as soon as they realised that they had been spotted.

We raced around to the other side of the field, unobserved by the running men, and met up with the other unit. We waited, as the fog was quite dense in the valley where we were and we could see very little across the field. We were waiting for sometime and I began to think that they must have turned off, when suddenly what I can only describe as an apparition appeared out of the mist and twelve men were running towards us.

On spotting us they slowed down and the language was blue, fortunately back-up had just arrived. The men were unable to verify who they were. When asked for their names and addresses, they all replied, "Bill Smiff, The Caravan site, Dagenham, guv'nor." They were all detained with their dogs but the Custody Sergeant at Saffron Walden Police Station was not amused when we arrived with twelve very muddy men and dogs, the latter were locked in the prisoners' exercise yard.

Enquiries then revealed that they were all from West Sussex and, as became the normal on this operation, two of the men were wanted by other police forces for much more serious offences. The two were later collected and all received substantial fines at court.

One Sunday morning we were to experience a particularly violent group of coursers. The morning had started fairly quietly and I uttered those fatal words, "Maybe we are going to have a quiet day." A call went up on the CB radio that a large gang of coursers had been spotted in a 100 acre field adjacent to the M11. We all headed to the location and on our arrival we could see a number of vehicles in the middle of the field of wheat which was about 5 cm high. We began to drive down a track towards them and on seeing us the men, who were some way from their cars, began running back towards them. We arrived just as the men, who were covered in mud, had arrived at their four wheel drives.

I approached one group of men but, as I did, all four jumped into one of the vehicles and roared off leaving deep ruts across the field. Myself and one of the gamekeepers jumped into our pick-up and gave chase. The car we were following weaved across the field and we followed close behind. Suddenly I saw a rear window open and a catapult appear - a loud crack on the windscreen made us realise that we were under fire. A number of shots rained in on us as we tried to take evasive action. A line of chips appeared right across the windscreen, which angered my gamekeeper driver. He was determined to stay with them while I called up for urgent assistance both on the police radio and the CB. We were heading towards a lane in front of a wood and I could see a convoy of keepers' vehicles heading towards us.

We continued to follow the vehicle as more chips appeared on the windscreen, one right in my sight line - if the missile had come through the screen it would have hit me in the face. The missiles were in fact ball bearings. As we approached the lane the car crashed through a hedge and bounced on to the lane surface narrowly missing the lead keeper's vehicle. We followed the vehicle as it roared off towards a motorway bridge. I then heard a two-tone siren and saw a police vehicle overtaking the convoy behind us; we slowed and let it in front of us. As we reached the motorway bridge and began to travel across it, the police vehicle pulled alongside the coursers' vehicle and then to my utter amazement the coursers' vehicle rammed the police vehicle, which responded by turning back into the other car to prevent being forced into the safety railings - the consequences of being forced through the railings were not worth thinking about.

Both vehicles came to a stop and everybody in the convoy leapt out, these coursers were going nowhere! All the keepers were big men and the Sergeant driving the police vehicle was 6' 4". I got the front passenger of the coursers' car out and he literally unwound out of the car, he towered over everyone. Other police vehicles, including a carrier, had arrived and I quickly arrested this giant and placed him in the carrier in handcuffs, he was a very angry man. As I left to take my prisoner to Saffron Walden Police Station traffic cars arrived to deal with the police accident, otherwise known in the job as a 'Polacc.'

Subsequent enquiries with Sussex Police, where my prisoner came from, revealed that he was well known to the local police in Lewes where he was a major drug dealer. There were a number of warrants out for his arrest and they were curious as to how we had got him in. Apparently he can be quite a handful, normally needing several police officers to arrest him, I think he had seen the size of some of our gamekeepers and, of course, our Sergeant!

All four men eventually appeared before Saffron Walden Magistrates Court charged with a number of offences including criminal damage to a standing crop of wheat (estimated £300 worth of damage), criminal damage to the keeper's vehicle, three of the four were charged with this offence as we could not prove who was firing the ball bearings, trespassing in pursuit of game (hare coursing), and the driver for reckless driving and other offences. All received substantial fines, compensation orders and costs, and the driver was banned from driving for twelve months.

This was one of the most serious cases that I dealt with under Operation Tortoise. The operation continued for many years until the message got through to the coursers' circle that if they coursed in Essex they would be detained, normally all day as it took ages to sort out their identification and addresses. A famous saying went through the coursing circles, "Don't course in Essex or you will have breakfast, dinner and tea with Essex Police."

A Pair Of Watchful Eyes

For the first few years that I was at Thaxted, the beat came under the Dunmow section. A new Sergeant arrived at Dunmow and became responsible for me and my beat. One spring morning he rang me and asked if he could come out with me for the morning to show him around. I collected him and we chatted as I showed him my area.

It soon transpired that he was a keen bird watcher and in fact had a few birds of prey of his own including a buzzard and a tawny owl - we were going to get on well! We drove around the beat and out into the very isolated areas. We travelled along a very narrow lane with open fields on either side and a partial hedge with the odd tree. As we rounded a bend and began to approach a low, pollarded willow tree, I said to the Sergeant, "If you look in the branches of this tree as we go past you will see a Little Owl peering out." The Sergeant's retort was, "Yeah, yeah, yeah," sarcastically.

As we drove past the tree, sure enough there were two bright yellow eyes glaring at us. The sergeant laughed and said, "Boy, you not only know your beat, you even know where the birds are." I smiled smugly as I drove on - I knew the bird would be there.

A Snake In The Kitchen

One morning I was off duty when I received a call from the control room at HQ. A terrified lady had rung in to report that her cat had brought a huge, live snake into her kitchen and it had disappeared under her fridge. It was quite a way away but I told control that I would attend in case the snake was a dangerous one.

I drove to the house and the lady called out from her front bedroom. She was terrified of snakes and would not come down and open the door to let me in. She told me that there was a key under the doormat so I let myself in and made my way to the kitchen. The bottom of the door had been blocked with a lot of papers and magazines, which I had to clear away before I could open the door; I did so cautiously.

To my relief I could not see any monster. With some trepidation I began to pull the fridge out and to my surprise I saw not a huge snake, but in fact a 9" long slowworm, which is not a snake but a harmless, legless lizard. It was a beautiful copper colour and I reached down and managed to pick it up without too much trouble. I checked it over but it appeared to be uninjured, despite the best efforts of the cat.

I took the slowworm away as I was concerned that if I released it in the garden, the cat might find it again. I released it in an area where I knew there were other slowworms and informed my control of the result - they had a little chuckle.

Spiders And Scorpions

One morning I was on duty with a colleague when we were sent to a dispute over a neighbour's boundary fence. We spoke to both parties and explained that this was not a police matter and would have to be resolved by their solicitors.

Whilst in one of the houses, I suddenly noticed a vivarium in the sitting room, which naturally roused my curiosity. As I approached the glass front I could see the contents - one large scorpion. I spoke to the lady who explained to me that she bred them! As I had expressed an interest, she showed me through to another room, where I was astounded to see about twenty vivaria containing huge spiders. The lady identified them to me as tarantulas, which she apparently bred as well.

It is amazing what you find sometimes when dealing with domestics.

Bones In The Bank

One Christmas an incident occurred that totally disrupted my festive celebrations. We had a bank in Town Street, Thaxted that was having some renovations carried out during the Christmas break. One aspect of these renovations was the cellar of the building, which had remained sealed for a very long time.

On Christmas Eve my wife and I were shopping for those last minute items before the shops close for the Christmas break. Soon after we got back the phone rang - it was police control. The builders working on the bank had put a 999 call in as they had discovered what they described as 'human remains' in the cellar. As this was a potential crime scene, it needed to be guarded and they asked if I would attend. I was supposed to be off over this Christmas, the first I was going to have off in a long time, but the bones put paid to that.

I went down to the scene where loads of officers were milling around from CID at HQ, Scenes of Crime Officers, and senior, uniformed officers. I decided to keep right out of the way and by early evening virtually everybody had gone, leaving me sitting outside in my police car. Several of the local residents brought me out cups of tea and mince pies and I was relieved at midnight by an officer from Dunmow.

After my children had opened their presents on Christmas morning and we had had breakfast, I went down to the bank to relieve the night shift officer. I remained there for the rest of the day in the ghost town. I was relieved at 22:00 after a twelve hour shift at the bank.

On Boxing Day the bones were examined by a pathologist who concluded that they were not human but were in fact pig bones! It transpired that the bones had originated from a butcher next door to the bank and had been brought to the cellar by rats a long time ago.

Happy Christmas!

A Plucky Owl

Late one winter evening there was a knock at the office door and I opened it to see a driver standing there holding a towel. He came in and placed the towel on the counter. I gently unravelled it and there lay a beautiful adult tawny owl. The gentleman had hit it hard in his car just outside Thaxted and had gone back and picked it up. My first impression was that it was dead but, as I examined it, I detected that it was still breathing. There was no blood and no obvious sign of injury so I gently placed it in a box to see if it would survive the night then left it in the office where it was quite warm.

Early the following morning, Cassie was barking at the office door between the house and the office. I went through and, to my amazement, the owl had got out of the box and was flying around the office - it had made a full recovery. Cassie was very wary of it as it glared down at her with total contempt. I decided to release it the following night - tawny owls do not like flying during daylight - and left it loose in the office, which was out of bounds for the day.

Typically, later that morning my Inspector rang to say that he was on his way over to see me. I explained to him about the owl but he decided to come over anyway. He arrived armed with a camera - he had never seen a wild tawny owl close up. The bird posed well for him on a perch that I had set up for the creature - this was not the first bird I had had flying around my office.

The following night I took the owl back to where it had been hit and released it. It is always a lovely moment when you release a wild bird back into its natural environment and it drifted off on silent wings into the darkness.

I rang the driver who had brought the bird in and told him what had happened. He was quite pleased that he had probably saved the bird's life by bringing it in, as another car may have finished it off or a fox may have taken it.

A Stubborn Bird

I was off duty one morning when I received a phone call from a local farmer who had a rather strange problem: he was in the process of ploughing a field near a wood and there was a bird sitting on the stubble in the middle of the field that was refusing to move! He asked for my help, and more out of curiosity than anything else, I agreed to pop over, as it was only a mile or so from Thaxted.

I was quite surprised to find that the bird was in fact a juvenile buzzard and sure enough it was refusing to move. Every time I approached it, the bird dropped it's head and puffed up its feathers in an aggressive stance. I spotted one of the adults in one of the trees watching me and the youngster, which was obviously one of hers. I was a little concerned that she might try and have a go at me if I tried to move the miscreant.

I took a towel from my Land Rover and approached the youngster, asking the farmer to watch the adult just in case she decided to swoop down on me. I quickly dropped the towel over the bird and picked it up carefully as their talons and beak are really sharp even at that early age. I carried the bird to the edge of the wood and, not without some difficulty, placed it on a branch of a tree - I was constantly aware of a pair of fierce eyes watching my every move from high in the trees above me.

I do believe that the young buzzard could fly but just couldn't be bothered!

Badgers

Badgers are one of the most easily recognised mammals, and to many are a very endearing sight, whilst to others a pest. In the UK since 1992, they have enjoyed a high level of legal protection under the Badger Act, which not only protects the animal itself but also the sett where they live. As a result of this protection the species made up a large part of my workload as a Police Wildlife Crime Officer. The next few stories are all true and involve badgers and the many exploits that they can get up to.

One major job that came in involved the eviction of a large group of badgers from under a huge, 17th century, Essex barn, which had Grade II listing. The barn was in a dilapidated state and was sinking due to all the excavations by the badgers over a period of many years. Essex County Council and English Heritage advised the farmer who owned the barn that he must bring the barn up to standard. The local badger group were contacted and they in turn contacted me. Along with the field officer for the local group, Dave Start, I attended the barn in early March with the owner, who I knew.

The first thing we needed to do was to confirm that the sett was occupied. That was not difficult as there were balls of bedding outside a number of entrances and fresh spoil. Dave was of the opinion that there were cubs in a number of the setts under this barn as badgers cub in February to March. The farmer had agreed that the group could build an artificial sett nearby and when the time was right we would 'evict' them. The first thing we needed to do was to apply to the court for an eviction order, serve it on the badgers, who after reading it had fourteen days to get out - I jest of course but this work would have to be carried out under licence from English Nature, now renamed Natural England. In case you are wondering why the badgers had to be moved, it was primarily due to the amount of damage they were causing both under and inside the barn, and in order for the barn to be restored scaffolding would have to be erected and the barn underpinned, resulting in severe interference and possible destruction of many parts of the sett.

I agreed to apply for the licence and after some discussions between government departments this was issued. One cold, but dry, weekend in April work began constructing the new sett. All the equipment to build the sett was donated by local companies, including the plastic tunnelling from a local water company. The plan was to build a number of chambers for the badgers which were constructed with railway sleepers bolted together with steel pins. One of the group members had a mini digger and dug out all the channels for the tunnels and the large squares for the chambers - that digger saved a lot of work.

The group worked tremendously hard throughout the weekend and by Sunday evening the Badger Hilton was complete. Before burying the chambers we placed dry straw in each chamber, though I wanted to put in showers, lights on timer switches ...! We threw peanuts up the pipes at either end and scattered a few around outside - badgers adore peanuts. Due to the fact that there were cubs under the barn there was nothing more to be done until October when it would be feasible to evict the badgers. Dave and I returned to the Hilton a week later to find all the peanuts gone and badger footprints inside the tunnels, curiosity had got the better of some of the badgers.

Dave and I visited the Hilton again in mid-July and it was quite apparent that some of the badgers had packed their suitcases and moved into their new luxury sett. All the bedding that we had put in had been removed by the occupants and replaced with their own bedding - we were very pleased. We decided that nothing more could be done until October but a number of gates, 21 in total, were made during the summer to go over each of the sett entrances at the barn. During the first weekend in October the gates were placed over each of the entrances but it was apparent from the debris and cobwebs in a lot of the entrances that quite a few of the occupants had already moved out and into their new sett where there was a lot of activity.

Within a few days of the gates going on all the badgers got the hint and moved out, except one old brock that had declared UDI and was refusing to move. Eventually even he was evicted and we had won. It had taken eleven months from the time the job came in to the last badger leaving. A lot of dedicated people were involved in this major sett relocation and I give talks on this major removal all over the country.

Another job involved a large family of badgers that had lived in an old Essex churchyard for a number of years without too many problems. However, as the family expanded the number of setts increased, a number of old graves were 'occupied' and the inevitable happened - bones began to appear on the surface, culminating in a skull appearing! The church authorities had had enough and the Department for Food and Rural Affairs (DEFRA) were contacted. Their local Wildlife Inspector contacted me and invited me along to a site visit to discuss the options.

The scene that greeted us was quite awesome. The graveyard was very old and had mature trees growing throughout. As we walked through we had to be very careful as there were sett entrances everywhere and it was obvious that a lot of the paths were undermined and could collapse under our weight. Many of the grave stones were either falling over or sinking with the graves that they were marking. Outside some of the sett entrances we found bones in amongst the spoil heaps, as well as in some of the bedding heaps outside some of the larger entrances.

It soon became apparent that this was going to be a major job as the badgers were going to have to be moved rather than evicted as there was nowhere for them to go. Thank goodness this was going to be a DEFRA job, and at the time I left the force it was still ongoing.

For many years Pat and I took a large display around the country showing the work of Police Wildlife Crime Officers. At one show we were exhibiting at Audley End House in Saffron Walden an unusual incident occurred. We set up our display in a huge marquee with a large number of other stalls. The next marquee to ours was the food marquee with various stalls and a cafeteria area inside.

Pat and I arrived early on the Saturday morning to put the finishing touches to our display, which comprised photographs, a big display of illegal traps, skins and plenty more. One of the organisers approached us and told us that an animal, believed to have been a dog had got into the food tent overnight and had wreaked havoc. Food had been spread everywhere, partially eaten pies were strewn all over the grass - I went with the organiser to have a look. The scene that greeted us was one of mayhem. People were rushing around clearing up all the mess. Somebody jokingly said, "Whoever or whatever it was must have a sweet tooth," a comment that was to have some relevance later on. From the mess I assumed that there must have been more than one animal.

The organisers checked all the stallholders and craft fair people who were staying on the site to see if (a) they had dogs and (b) if they were loose last night, the result was negative. The following night someone remained in the food tent all night on security duty and the intruder(s) did not return.

Halfway through the Sunday morning the grounds and gardens were packed with visitors. One of the members of staff from the house came rushing up to me and reported seeing what appeared to be an injured badger, with a possible open wound on its rear end, in the flower beds at the back of the house. I immediately reported the matter to the local Badger Protection Group who had a stall in another marquee. We made a search of the gardens but couldn't find it and I began to wonder if this was the creature responsible for the 'break in' in the food tent, however, I couldn't believe that one animal could cause such devastation.

We then received another report that the animal was rummaging around under a huge Cedar of Lebanon tree at the southern end of the house. The badger group fetched a large cage to catch it and food, including peanuts, which badgers love, was placed inside - the trap was set. We found the badger under the tree and placed the cage nearby. The animal appeared very weak and did indeed have a nasty wound on its rear end. It didn't take much encouragement as we gently coaxed it towards the cage. As soon as it picked up the scent of the food in the cage it was in like a shot. We then examined the animal and could see the remains of fruit pie on its flanks, my suspicions were confirmed! It was very weak and its injuries were consistent with the animal having had a fight with another badger, not uncommon in badger society.

The animal was taken back to the 'badger hospital' in Thaxted which was run by Dave and Penny Start, where it was treated for its injuries and fed up over a period of seven days. She was then brought back to the Audley End Estate and I assisted in her release near to the sett where it was believed she had come from. She ran out of the box and scuttled off into the long grass, where she stopped and looked around at Dave and I before disappearing into the bushes. It was a lovely moment, as I have said before it is always lovely when you can release a creature back into the wild where they belong.

One evening Pat and I were having a meal when the phone rang. A very upset lady was on the phone - she had hit a badger on a road a few miles from our house. The badger was lying in the middle of the road and was seriously injured. I told the lady not to touch it or try and move the poor creature, as it could injure her. I told her that I would get someone to her and rang my control to ask them to get someone to the lady. I also rang the local badger group and they said that they would attend - there was nothing more that I could do.

The following morning I learnt that the lady had ignored my advice and had tried to move the injured animal. The badger had bitten hard into the woman's right hand severing an artery; she had ended up in intensive care at Addenbrooke's hospital and had been kept in overnight. I always advise people that if you injure a badger, do not approach it or try and move it because if they are injured and terrified, they are powerful creatures that will strike out at anything.

I learnt this lesson the hard way when I was a youngster and I tried to pick up what I thought was a dead stoat (a close relative of the badger family). I soon learnt that it was alive when it bit hard and deep into my left thumb muscle. It was very painful and needed three stitches, which left me with a permanent scar – a lesson I was never to forget!

A fruit farmer friend of mine rang me one morning concerning a problem badger. On his farm he had about four acres of Pick Your Own strawberries on a slope leading down to a river. On the river bank there was a badger sett. Now it was known that the badgers were helping themselves to strawberries at night, and the farmer was prepared to tolerate this - as he said there was nothing he could do anyway. However, this particular year the badgers had overstepped the mark and had dug a sett right in the middle of the strawberries - why walk all that way when we could have them on tap, was obviously the thought on the badgers' minds!

This posed a serious problem for the farmer for the sett was protected under the 1992 Badger Protection Act but it was going to be a major hazard to the public whilst they were picking strawberries, hence the call to me. We decided to fence the sett off during the day while the badgers were underground and remove the fence every night to allow the badgers to feed.

This routine continued for seven weeks until the strawberries were finished and the badgers moved out and back to their main sett. Large cobwebs formed over the sett entrance suggesting that there was no activity and in the autumn the sett was filled in. However, the following year at the beginning of the strawberry season the badgers were back to the same spot. It would appear that this routine will continue until the strawberry bed is ploughed up at the end of its productive life!

A female badger will normally give birth in late February/early March and at this time will often evict the dominant male as he can pose a threat to the cubs. The poor old brock would go off and try and find somewhere to live for a few months until the cubs were old enough to fend for themselves. Often the brock would dig a sett in some awkward spots, most likely in a field with young wheat or barley in East Anglia and I was called in to advise. A typical scenario would be that the badger would dig down 9' or more and add a chamber at the bottom in one night, as that is where he believes he is going to live for a few months. The land owner has now got a problem because the sett is protected under the Badger Act. If the badger is to be moved a licence is required for him to be evicted but one of the problems is that we have no control over where he goes and of course there is nothing to stop him going 50 yards up the field and digging in again, which often happens.

Although I am a great champion of badgers, I am very aware of the damage they can cause and the problems they can create. Having said that, to sit outside a sett in May and watch both adults and cubs come out and play has got to be one of the wonders of nature. A very determined badger in Rayleigh caused a desperate lady to contact DEFRA, who in turn contacted me. I called on the lady with a DEFRA Inspector to assess the situation, although I did not think there was a lot we could do. The situation was simply that the lady lived on a small estate on the outskirts of Rayleigh, with open scrub and woodland behind her house. In this wooded area there was a large and well-established badger sett. For some reason that was not immediately apparent, the badgers had smashed through a wooden fence panel and entered her garden. However, the badgers were not remaining in the lady's garden but were crossing her lawn and pushing through a thick hedge into the neighbour's garden where they were being fed.

The lady had replaced her fence panel four times after the badgers had bust through each time. The lady had asked her neighbour to stop feeding the miscreants but she had refused as she loved to see them. The lady was not complaining against badgers but she objected to the damage that they were causing.

We sat and had a cup of tea with the lady and discussed the options, which were few. Moving the sett was not an option. I suggested feeding the badgers outside the fence, but that was not an option. Eventually we suggested to the lady that she might install a gate on the hole, similar to a cat flap type assembly, to allow the badgers in and out.

The gate was installed and the badgers used it - the badgers and the lady were both happy - problem resolved.

One night I was working as acting Sergeant at Dunmow. I was out on patrol with a female officer; it had been a quiet night and we were about to return to the police station for a cup of tea. We had been talking about badgers and it transpired that my colleague had never seen a live badger, but that was about to change quite unexpectedly. We were travelling along a road in a remote area, approaching an isolated cottage. As we got closer I suddenly spotted a black and white character on the grass verge by the gate of the cottage. I stopped and we watched as the creature moved towards the gate, oblivious to our presence. My colleague was speechless and watched, spellbound.

Then something quite remarkable happened. The badger reached the gate and stopped - I thought for a moment it was going to barge straight through the wooden gate, but it didn't. It sat down in front of the gate and then sat back on its haunches, lifted its front feet up and gently leaned against the gate which then opened. The badger disappeared through the gate and out of sight. I looked at my colleague who was speechless - the badger had obviously learnt this technique but I wondered if the cottage occupants knew of their visitor.

When we got back to the station at midnight my colleague was full of it, she could not believe what she had seen. The following night she pleaded with me to visit the cottage again, so after dealing with a road accident we popped down to the cottage but there was no sign of our caller. I turned the car around and as we came up to the cottage, we suddenly saw our friend trot across the road ahead of us, up onto the verge and up to the gate. Almost without stopping it sat up and repeated its trick from the previous night before disappearing through the gate.

That was the last time we saw him, for although he was obviously visiting this cottage on a fairly regular basis, we never timed our arrival right again.

Another evening I was off duty at home when I answered the phone. A gentleman was enquiring as to how he could stop badgers coming into his garden centre and digging up his flower beds, as the damage they were causing was tremendous. After speaking to him for quite a while it became apparent exactly what was happening. We were experiencing a particularly dry summer and the badgers' staple diet is worms. Of course in dry weather worms disappear, normally going deep under ground but the owner of this garden centre was watering all his beds every day keeping the worms near the surface. Badgers, not being stupid, had discovered this source of food and were coming in every night to feast.

I had not come across this problem before so I had to think fairly quickly, as the gentleman was desperate for some sound advice. He knew where the badgers were coming in from. There were fields and hedges behind his premises and they were coming through the fence. I knew that it would be pointless to try and block the area where they were coming in as badgers are very determined creatures and would simply find another entrance.

I suddenly came up with an idea which was a real shot in the dark. I suggested to him that he might try feeding the badgers behind his property to discourage them from coming in. I suggested that he put peanuts and anything sweet out for them - badgers adore peanuts and of course they do have a sweet tooth. I really did not know if it would work or not but it was worth a try and I asked him to let me know the result.

The gentleman rang me about a month later, absolutely delighted that my suggestion had worked. He had placed out food for them every evening and once had taken his two grandchildren to a spot where they had a wonderful experience watching four badgers feeding. He wrote a letter of thanks to my Chief Constable, who was more than a little bemused.

Badgers are quite remarkable creatures and in these few stories I hope I have given the reader an insight into some of their antics.

The Joys Of Public Speaking

I began public speaking soon after I moved to Thaxted, initially just on nature conservation, using my own slides. I was giving about five or six talks a year and now, thirty years on, I am now giving over 200 annually travelling the length and breadth of the UK. I have a range of fourteen talks, all within the wildlife scenario, including 'Jersey Zoo and the work of Gerald Durrell', 'The Role of a Police Wildlife Crime Officer', 'Badgers', 'Wild Flowers', 'Birds', 'Seasons of a Woodland', 'Pond and River Life', 'A Celebration of Trees', 'Landscapes of Britain', 'Coastal wildlife and Landscapes' to list but a few. I talk to many varied and diverse groups from Women's Institutes, Gardening Clubs, Camera Clubs, University of the Third Age Groups, Colleges and Universities and anyone else who is interested. After a wonderful cruise deep into the

Arctic Circle in 2007, a new talk for the 2008 season is 'The Wildlife and Landscapes of the Arctic.' I took 2,300 slides on the trip!

Many amusing incidents have occurred during my public speaking career and the next few stories, all of which are true, are just a sample of some of my experiences over 30 years of public speaking.

Parking at the venue can often be an issue, particularly if space is limited. I carry quite a lot of display material, books, a range 70 greetings cards, a large card stand, plus a screen, table and projector, which all have to be unloaded and I like to be as close as possible to the entrance to the venue.

On one occasion I was due to give an afternoon talk to a ladies' group. As usual I had arrived early to get a good parking spot outside the entrance to the new village hall, which had a huge newly tarmacked car park with the potential to hold 200 cars. I sat and ate my lunch, happy in the thought that this was going to be an easy venue to unload into.

Later a large saloon drove into the car park, with a very elegant, well dressed lady driving it. The car pulled alongside my Land Rover and the lady indicated for me to wind down my window, which I did. She asked me in a very posh voice, "Can I help you?" With a smile I said, "I am giving a talk here this afternoon." She said, "I am the president, would you mind moving? You are parked in my parking space." I was a little surprised as the entire car park was otherwise empty! I indicated all the equipment in the back and said, "I would rather not as I have this lot to unload." It was as if she was not listening to me and she repeated, "You are in my parking space." I asked her, "Have you got stuff to unload?" and she replied, "No, but that is beside the point. You are in my parking space." Keeping my cool, just, I said, "Look lady, I have all this heavy equipment to unload, the car park is empty, I don't care who you are but I am not moving." She then came out with a classic, "After you have unloaded, can you move?" To which I replied, "If I move, it will be out of this car park and home, which will mean that you will not have a speaker this afternoon and I will send you a bill." At that point she roared off in a huff and parked in the car park; she did not speak to me for the rest of the afternoon.

To allow for the hard of hearing, I am often provided with a radio microphone, particularly for some of the larger groups. On one occasion I was talking to a large group with an audience of over 300 and was fitted with the microphone (a lapel mike). At half time we broke for a cup of tea and I went to the toilet, singing as I do. When I returned and walked down the aisle towards the stage, everybody stood up and clapped me. I was totally surprised and asked the chairman what was going on. He said, "You left your mike on, Pavarotti!" It takes a lot to embarrass me but I must admit that I had to chuckle.

On another occasion I was an after-lunch speaker to a gentlemen's group, with an average age in excess of 70. They had organised a couple of beers at the bar and a very nice meal. It was quite warm in the hall and I was due to begin after the meal. The lights went out and the slides began. I kept my voice fairly loud to keep them awake, as I suspected they may fall asleep. Within ten minutes of starting I was talking to a sea of bald heads, not one face out of the 80 gentlemen present was looking at me. I could have quite easily flashed through the slides in five minutes and finished and no-one would have been any the wiser, but I didn't. Remarkably I received a loud applause at the end despite the fact that no-one was actually watching the presentation!

I arrived at a hall in Hertfordshire for an evening talk to a camera club and was nice and early as usual. The talk was due to start at 20:00 but by 19:45 there was still no-one at the hall. I began to think that something was not quite right and rang the contact number that I had. There was no reply and by 20:10 I was still alone. I was just about to leave and drive the forty miles home when a car came roaring up - it was one of the club members, apparently they had changed the venue but had forgotten to tell me!

A very sad incident occurred at another talk that I was giving in London. I had arrived early and soon afterwards an old boy turned up and let me in. He did not look at all well and was out of breath as he struggled to put the chairs out. I helped him and he sat right at the back of the hall. When we broke for tea half way through the presentation, he came up and bought a couple of my greetings cards. At the end I was busy packing everything away as the hall cleared of people. The old boy appeared to be asleep at the back - nothing unusual during my talks. The chairman had been talking to me and said, "I suppose I had better wake George up, he usually drops off." He couldn't wake him so I rushed over but could not find a pulse and he was not breathing. I rang for an ambulance and started to try and resuscitate him but when the paramedics arrived they declared that he was dead. The committee were quite shocked, as this was the first time that anything like this had happened to them.

Sadly the same scenario was to recur not long afterwards when I was talking to a large group of senior citizens. Halfway through the presentation a voice shouted out in the dark, "Does anyone have a mobile phone?" I initially thought she meant that a mobile was ringing, although I always ask for them to be switched off during my talks. No-one responded and the lady then shouted again, "Has anyone got a mobile phone? I need an ambulance." I grabbed my phone and rang for an ambulance as the lights went up. Paramedics arrived but it was too late, the old boy appeared to have had a massive heart attack. The lady that had shouted out was sitting next to him and was a retired doctor.

On another occasion a gentleman went into a diabetic coma and fell off his chair. I thought that this was going to be the third but he was okay after paramedics revived him and everybody was quite relieved.

There is a saying 'Once a policeman, always a policeman.' I don't know if that is true but an incident occurred at one of my talks after I had retired that may reflect that saying. The venue was a large hall in the middle of a park with a huge play area. As I unloaded the equipment, I saw a large group of youngsters who had congregated near the swings and slides on the other side of the park. I didn't take a lot of notice, however, half way through the talk there was a loud bang and a window in the hall shattered. I ran outside and around the side of the building where a youth was holding a rifle. He went to run but I was at full pelt and rugby-tackled him where he stood - a tackle worthy of an England shirt. While I was on top of him, I got the gun away. Some of the ladies had come out and I asked one of them to dial 999. The cavalry soon arrived and the youth was taken away. I had to make a statement in the hall, while the ladies continued with their club business. Afterwards I apologised to the ladies that we were not going to be able to finish the presentation. They were more than happy, and had thoroughly enjoyed the 'entertainment'. One was heard to say, "We have never had so much excitement at one of our meetings, can he come back again?" I did return about a year later and there was no excitement.

It all happens at my talks, even my equipment can fail dramatically. At one talk, the first thing that happened was that halfway through the presentation, all the power went out. I jokingly said, "Haven't we put enough money in the meter?" It turned out to be closer to the truth than I could have imagined. The meter had run out, which was then followed by a desperate search for £1 coins. When the power returned everything went back to normal but the blackout had obviously upset the projector. About 15 minutes later, one of the audience called out to me, "Barry, there is smoke coming out of your projector." I rushed over to the power supply and switched it off. When the lights came on there was still smoke coming out of the back of the projector. There was obviously a serious problem inside but luckily I always carry a spare projector and the show went on.

A Crumbly Speaker

One Friday, quite recently, I was asked to give a talk to a pensioner group at a large company in Hertfordshire. I have spoken to this group on a number of occasions in the past.

The hall where the talks take place is part of a large social club with a bar and the hall itself is next to the restaurant. I had arrived early and set up my display, books, screen and projector. I was sitting in the restaurant having had a bite to eat and had left the door open to the hall so that I could keep an eye on my display.

A couple of young workers, who I soon learnt were analysts, came and sat on the table next to me. They were laughing and joking and discussing what they were all doing for the weekend. One of the group suddenly spotted my display and they all looked up. They could clearly see the blown-up picture of the cover of "The Wildlife Man" which is of me in uniform with a camera and Burt the badger. One of them said, "What's going on in there?" Another replied, "Oh that's the pensioners club, they meet in there and have some crumbly old speaker." I had my back to them and had to chuckle to myself.

I got up from my table and walked past the group. As I did so I leaned over and said, "I am the crumbly speaker for the pensioners." There was a deathly hush and a lot of very red faces. Nobody uttered a word as I disappeared into the hall and closed the door.

There were about 70 people in the audience and at the end of the talk I relayed this story to them, they were all in hysterics – I had made their day!

A Slide Show To Remember

O ne morning I was working an early turn and was due to be giving a talk to a local group at 14:30 on Seasons of a Woodland. The morning had been fairly quiet but all that was about to change when a robbery came in at a local shop and I attended immediately.

Two men wearing balaclavas had gone into the shop armed with a sledgehammer and threatened the staff behind a glass panel, which shattered with the force of the hammer. The men made off with a large quantity of cash and other items. The staff were in a state of severe shock and were understandably very distressed. I spent some time comforting them and by the time the cavalry arrived the men had gone. Their car, which was stolen from Harlow, was found on the forecourt of a local public house where they had switched vehicles.

CID and SOCO arrived and it soon became apparent that I was not going to get off at 14:00. I rang Pat and asked her to contact the group to tell them what had happened and to advise them that I would not be able to make the talk. Pat knew that I hated letting people down and it seldom happened, so foolishly she offered to stand in for me.

I eventually got off at 17:00 but the good news was that the two men were in custody at Harlow Police Station, having been arrested by Harlow officers in a second stolen car after a high speed chase around Harlow. All of the cash, along with the sledgehammer, was on board.

When I got home Pat greeted me with a beaming smile. She had completed the talk but there was a hitch – many of the slides were upside down and the talk had descended into a hilarious performance on "Seasons of an Australian wood" – I had forgotten that I had been sorting out this talk … oops!

A few months later I was talking to the same group and they all remembered the fabulous talk that Pat had given them. They wanted her back – I have competition!

As you can see, I have been very lucky throughout my working career, being able to follow my deep love of nature and the natural world. In 2003, I gained a prestigious award when I was named 'Wildlife Law Enforcer of the Year' by the World Wildlife Fund. This is an award presented annually to either a Police Wildlife Officer or a Customs and Excise Wildlife Officer who is considered to have made the most significant contribution to wildlife law enforcement.

In May 2007, I was made a Fellow of the British Naturalists Association at a ceremony in London, with Sir David Attenborough presenting the awards and receiving a lifetime achievement award himself. It was a wonderful moment for me when my wife Pat managed to get a photograph of the two of us, as I have always admired Sir David, since meeting him at Jersey Zoo many years ago, for all his work championing the natural world, going right back to my childhood.

I am very proud and humbled to have received these awards.

So there you have it, I hope you have enjoyed some of the stories in this book – there are many more! I hope I have not offended or upset anyone as that was not my intention.

As you have probably gathered a police officer really is a 'Jack Of All Trades' and a sense of humour is essential.